I0102251

Platform of Hope

Ideas Both Conservatives and Liberals Can Love

Timothy Bult

To my father, who inspired open-minded politics,
in search of solutions rather than criticism.

TABLE OF CONTENTS

1: A CANADIAN IN AMERICA

I'm a Canadian in the US. Our reputation for being "nice" might help with the challenge I tackle in this book. I wish to offer a useful political platform for American federal politics that is exciting and desirable for both conservatives and liberals. There are plenty of books preaching to the converted on either side, but I'm trying to gather and generate ideas that appeal to both.

Being Canadian made me an outsider to American politics, but hopefully an appealing kind of outsider. I have lived in Milwaukee, Wisconsin since 2014, paying US taxes, and very much enjoying life in the United States. I have had the good fortune to visit 38 states (plus DC), some on business, some as a tourist. I am grateful and happy to live here, and plan to get to all 50 states as soon as possible. On Thursday, February 8, 2024 I became an American citizen, in a moving ceremony where the judge talked about his immigrant grandparents, celebrated the 58 people becoming citizens that day, from 27 different countries, here in the Midwest. He encouraged us to maintain our cultures and traditions from our original countries, and to learn more about the other cultures we're blessed with. He said this is key to what makes America wonderful.

I am also Dutch, in the sense that both my parents were born in Groningen, a small city in the northeast corner of the Netherlands. This partially explains why I love to argue politics. Ask the Dutch what they think about any topic, and they are prone to check what you believe first, so they can take the opposite side, vociferously. I have fierce opinions against extremist policies from both the Democrats and the Republicans, but this book is not about criticizing one or the other. My goal here is to solve America's problems, with proposals that both Democrats and Republicans can love.

I kept this mantra in mind throughout the writing and rewriting of this book: I want both Republicans and Democrats, liberals and conservatives, to read this book without throwing it against the wall in rage, and in fact to love it. In today's climate, that is difficult. I know Republicans who get 100% of their news from Fox or even further right, who call CNN the Communist News Network. Anything positive said about Democratic politics can set them off. I also know Democrats who cannot watch five minutes of Fox without apoplexy, who will castigate me for pointing out anything positive about Trump's presidency. Can I really write an entire political book that both a Democrat and a Republican would read cover to cover? Can I proffer anything that both might agree to, and see as good prescriptions for the country?

I believe so, and here is why. The US is a wonderfully open nation. Its Constitution and subsequent evolution of its government have made it a bastion of liberty, one of the greatest champions of enlightenment values worldwide. America is the most desired home of emigrants. Although Canada and Australia take more immigrants as a percentage of population, the US has far more applicants in absolute terms. Why? Because it is a terrific country. As Leonard Cohen said, democracy "is coming to America first, the cradle of the best and of the worst". People are drawn to it. America is keen to be the best, and to change as needed to maintain a top ranking, on almost any score card you put in front of them.

Yes, America is horribly polarized right now, and it's difficult to pass any major legislation. Every government this century has struggled to get its election platform implemented, blocked by the Senate filibuster and both parties voting as a bloc instead of the individual conscience and judgment of the elected. And yet, while blocked legislation makes the news, Congress and our Presidents have continued to sign new bills into law. How many would you guess? Sure, some are pretty small and tame. But in the two years every Congress runs between elections, the lowest number of bills passed this century was 284, from January 2011 to January 2013. Every other Congress this century has passed more, averaging about 200 per year, despite the polarization. That's about 2 million words of bipartisan legislation per year. Wikipedia's list of "major legislation" has about 20 bills per year, year after year including throughout the Obama and Trump administrations. Work is getting done. The polarization has not actually ground the US to a halt, or at least not yet.

Although I have traveled around this wonderful country throughout my life, it is during these last ten years living here that the extremes have struck me so hard. The things I admire about America fill many pages, and the problems I lament and wish I could help solve can fill just as many.

Do Republicans want to hear about soaring government debt? Do Democrats want to hear about the Second Amendment? Or the right to life? Yes, I'm walking those mine fields, and hope that you will find my path interesting and useful, that you'll see my suggested solutions for America's problems much in America's spirit: centered on constitutional rights, personal freedom, free markets, and reduced government.

I have Trump-supporting friends, as well as Trump-hating friends, and I discuss politics with all of them, whoever shows the slightest interest, at every opportunity. I have addressed all the problems and criticisms I can collect, to make this platform complete and balanced. In that vein, I talk about appropriate controls on immigration. I talk about keeping a strong military, the right to life in the context of abortion, the height of our taxes, and the growing government debt. I talk about all the issues dear to Democrats, and all the issues dear to Republicans. If you care about America, I think you should listen to the other side, as well as your own. Don't just watch Fox. Don't just read the New York Times. Read both sides.

In 2019 I asked a friend who votes for Trump why he did so. He affirmed he'd be voting for Trump again in 2020. Here is the text he sent me: "He is killing it. Great economy. Stock market crazy. No war. Building the wall." If you measure Trump, even through the Covid-19 pandemic, by GDP growth, the Dow or S&P500, reducing US involvement in wars, and reduction of Mexican immigrants, he was indeed a success, and his fans continue to applaud him for it. My Republican friends' other priorities usually include preventing abortion, keeping their right to have guns, lower taxes, and lower regulation. The ideas in this book address all these, with policies I think Democrats will like, while at the same time giving Democrats what they want. How? Read on.

A friend pointed out that I have no credentials to write this book. One of my sons has a degree in Political Science and works in the bureaucracy of the Province of British Columbia, but that's as close to politics or government as I've come, other than reading and thinking and talking with people. The same friend did say that free speech is one of the wonderful things about the US, and that many presidents have been relatively clueless about how to run a country, so the opinions of a reasonably well traveled and well-read non-politician might be useful anyway. While my weaknesses as a political pundit for are therefore obvious, please humor me while I tell you a little more about myself, why I've attempted this book, and what value my perspective might have.

One major weakness, particularly for addressing issues like racism, or abortion, is that I'm an extremely fortunate, privileged white man. I did not have to overcome any adversity to get a wonderful education and a rewarding career. I studied hard and graduated top of my high school in the small town of Trail, British Columbia, but I did it out of an excessive ego and a crazy hunger for reading books and knowing everything, not because my life would be miserable otherwise. I went to the University of British Columbia, in Vancouver, because it was the obvious choice for a local BC boy. I only learned later that UBC is ranked in the top 50 universities worldwide. I got a degree in Computer Science because computers were fun, and this led to a well-paying career. The world was handed to me. Perhaps better ideas will come from someone who had to struggle harder.

A second weakness is that I have a biased point of view. Everyone does, but mine is challenging for the purposes of this book. Compared to the average American, I'm a liberal, somewhat to the left of America's political center, at least socially if not financially. Perhaps that will make it impossible for me to write ideas that American conservatives will love – but I am sincerely trying. If you are conservative, and you feel I've written something incorrect or offensive to your values, please let me know. Thanks to your feedback, I hope my revisions to this book get ever closer to my goal.

I grew up in a country where everyone has access to excellent health care and education, so I struggle to relate to politicians who don't believe in these. I'm a scientist and businessman, so I struggle to relate to extremists who are anti-science or anti-business or otherwise irrational. I am inveterately meliorist, so I struggle to understand pessimists and cynics. But I will do my very best to appeal to all rational and moderate Americans, and maybe even the somewhat extreme. I strongly believe in capitalism, which will alienate me from extremists on the left end of the spectrum. I have to accept I will lose readers at both extremes and hope I can offer rewarding ideas for the 40% on either side of the American center. I'd be happy with 80%.

I do have a few good points toward writing a useful political platform. First, I've lived in Canada, France, and the US, and always been curious about how government worked, asking lots of questions and reading as much as I could. My job and a travel bug brought me to China, Vietnam, Hong Kong, England, Scotland, Tahiti, Bora Bora, the United Arab Emirates, Israel, much of the Caribbean, Switzerland, Costa Rica, South Korea, Panama, Morocco, Portugal, Spain, Italy, Japan, Mexico, and Greece. For a couple years, I spent more time working out of London hotels than my own home in Vancouver, and traveled all over the UK, on projects for local governments. For another few years, I was back and forth to Israel, and traveled to every corner of that fascinating country, including some time in the Palestinian Territories. Wherever I travel, I'm curious about how people live, what rights they have, how they feel and behave, what their government is like, how they got where they are. I feel richer every time I visit a new country, just as I feel richer with knowledge every time I visit a new state in the US. So far, I've been from California to Maine, from Florida to Washington, from Alaska to Hawaii, from the Deep South to the farthest North, from red Texas to blue New York. Wherever I go in the US, I probe with curiosity at the political attitudes, the standards of living, the positives, and the problems. Of course lots of people have traveled more than I have, but I think I've exposed myself to a wide range of ways to run a country, and tried to learn from all of them, whether great ideas to try, or horrible mistakes to avoid.

In addition to my travels, I've been a bookworm my whole life. I grew up in Fruitvale, British Columbia, a tiny village, and we lived over a mile from the center of town. My nearest friend lived half a mile away. I had a lot of time to read. Throughout high school, I tried to read a book a day, and sometimes succeeded. Books give you lots of ideas, good and bad. I read Karl Marx's Communist Manifesto, with its fascinating insights and terrible prescriptions. I've subscribed to The Economist for decades and read it thoroughly every week. I have a library of business and macroeconomics books thanks to a career in business. I read the Bible, the Book of Mormon, most of Shakespeare, lots of Victorian novels. I devoured the entire science fiction collection of our local library, and later bought a wall full of my own. I'm not saying Asimov's Three Laws of Robotics are enough basis for designing a utopian society, but going from Ayn Rand to Heinlein to Aldous Huxley certainly helped open my eyes to a range of possibilities.

My education at universities in Canada and France was eclectic. I applied to study in France on a whim, and was accepted. I was happy and surprised to learn that French universities charged no tuition, even to foreign students. I earned a *"Maitrise d'Informatique"* (Master's of Computer Science) for an administrative fee of about $10. Back in Canada I finished a Master's Degree in Artificial Intelligence, but along the way I took courses in the Biblical and Classical Roots of English Literature, three years of Mandarin Chinese, Quantum Physics, Relativity, Chemistry, and a few advanced Maths. I think these helped to open my mind, taught me to think logically, and communicate with people all over the world more effectively. There are American politicians and pundits with more impressive intelligence and education, but I think I learned enough to form some useful opinions.

None of this would matter for this book, without a passion for politics. All my life, I fantasized about someday solving the world's deepest problems. From what I've seen around the world, the structure and policies and leaders of national governments have enormous impact on whether people live well or miserably. I care deeply that more people thrive, that fewer people suffer and die too young. Some countries with no natural resources, no obvious reason to be rich, become incredibly healthy and wealthy and happy—Denmark, for example. Some countries with every advantage, abundant natural resources and educated populations, become hell houses of poverty and torture—Venezuela and Iran, for example. In the middle is my new home, the United States, which features the very best that humankind has created, while

7

in a few ways scraping the bottom of the civilized world[1]. I want my new home to thrive even more, and I'm thrilled to spend some years of my best efforts to gather these ideas, and offer them to my neighbors, and hope to make America even greater than it is today.

There are occasionally times that one party holds the Presidency as well as the House and Senate. If they do not hold 60 Senate seats, they can still pass tax and spending legislation without the other party. But for anything else, and the majority of the time, legislation requires votes from both parties to pass.

Each of the following chapters examines a hot issue in American politics. There is a chapter on every issue on the average top ten list for any conservative or liberal in the country. For each, I try to summarize the issue, give some factual context to understand it, and then offer a bipartisan American solution. I'm focused on what the US federal government can and should do, in ways that all of you will love. For issues where I've failed that goal, I hope you'll forgive my veering too far to one side or the other, and at least join me in seeking bipartisan compromise.

---

1 For example, by some measures of health care quality, the US ranks lowest of 11 rich nations, despite spending the most. www.commonwealthfund.org/press-release/2014/us-health-system-ranks-last-among-eleven-countries-measures-access-equity

2: MILITARY SPENDING

I would love a world where the values I hold most dear are protected in every country, for everybody:

- **Democracy**: the regular, peaceful, and planned turnover of government, with the right for anyone to promote a new party, a new leader, a new platform, and the right for everyone to have an equal vote in the regular decision to renew.

- **Free Speech**: the right for everyone to say or publish whatever they want, with very few limits.

- **Free Press**: journalists who criticize the government and expose crime must be supported, and not repressed.

- **Free Market**: the right for people and their companies to innovate, to buy or sell what they want, to compete and win and make money, because that motivation to make money leads to ever rising quality of life, as people work hard to sell what other people want.

- **Property Rights**: the right to own something. If you own it, the government should support you if someone steals it from you. This may sound obvious, because it's a right we take for granted in western democracies, but it is trampled on or ignored in too many places, and under threat from extremists on both the right and left.

- **Right to Life**: governments should prevent, rather than condone or conduct ethnic cleansing, killings, or any other form of ending human life.

- **Personal Freedom**: if it doesn't harm another human being, and you want to do it, you should have the right to do so. You should be allowed to own, shoot, say, write, eat, and do whatever you like. To most Westerners, this seems obvious, but again, personal freedoms are scorned and denied around the world. People who want to worship are oppressed by atheists or people of another faith. People are killed for having sex with whom they choose.

- **Independent Judiciary**: judges must not be controlled by politicians. Laws must be applied consistently by people devoted to human rights, as expressed in constitutions and democratically passed laws. When judges become political, tyranny follows closely.

Why do I discuss these human rights in a chapter on the US Military? Because there is a fundamental war of values under way on Earth, and military strength is one of the essential factors that will determine who wins that war. I was going to write that there are two sides to this war, but to recognize the more complex reality, I think it's worth thinking of three groups. Any such classification is a simplification, and most human beings will support different fractions of all these views, but I find them a useful way to think of the political powers in the world today:

1.   The fans of **Democracy**. This is the side who believes in the primacy of all the rights I list above. We believe life gets better and better, thanks to personal rights and freedoms. In my opinion, the most important of these rights to defend is the right to vote, because without it, tyrants eventually take over, and trample on the other rights. Most Americans are on this side. Most people on Earth are firmly on this side, in every country[2].

2.   The **Dictators**. Of course they don't call themselves that. Their names for themselves are things like "enlightened leaders" or "beloved leaders" or "The Party" or "Loyalists" or "National Pride". The strongest and best example today is the Chinese Communist Party, and its many fans. They can point to tremendous achievements. For example, China's government in the last 50 years has raised almost a billion people out of extreme poverty[3], and arguably done more to raise global standards of living than any other country. They have avoided war for over 50 years. These achievements are real, and such governments develop a powerful fan base. The problem, which history teaches again and again, is that

---

2 "More than half in each of the nations polled consider representative democracy a very or somewhat good way to govern their country." Of course the degree of commitment varies by country, and over time, but no other system enjoys as much support as democracy.

www.pewresearch.org/global/2017/10/16/globally-broad-support-for-representative-and-direct-democracy/

3 "Deep-sixing poverty in China", The Brookings Institute (Jan 25, 2021),

https://www.brookings.edu/blog/future-development/2021/01/25/deep-sixing-poverty-in-china/. The article actually argues China should be doing better, for its level of wealth, but the disagreement is over poverty vs. extreme poverty.

without democracy, even the best of such governments slide toward repression and oppression, and eventually massive death and destruction. See Hitler, Mussolini, Stalin, the Kim's of North Korea, and the misery of Venezuela. Most of these began with idealistic visions and benefits for their people[4], before giving in to the temptations of absolute power. This is most dangerously true of China today, where the enlightened dictatorship of the post-Mao party is giving way to the raw power dictatorship of Xi Jinping, and mass oppression is steadily turning China into a prison state[5].

3. The **Socialists**. I almost called this side the Communists, or the Far Left, or the Woke. This is the side of many idealistic youth around the world. Any classification of humans is a simplification, a generalization that won't hold for lots of examples, but hopefully has some value to capture useful trends. I think of this group as the people who demand saving the planet from global warming as a top priority, along with reducing income and wealth inequality. They tend to view large corporations and most governments as their enemy, since those organizations have led to today's inequality and environmental risk. I distinguish them from the Democrats because their idealistic priority is saving the world, rather than the more conservative priority to preserve democratic rights. Most socialists believe in democracy, but I think there's a danger that if democracy doesn't

---

4 For one example of an idealistic beginning, review the early years of Hugo Chavez' presidency of Venezuela, elected and supported by the population:

https://www.britannica.com/place/Venezuela/The-Hugo-Chavez-presidency

5 https://www.nytimes.com/2019/08/31/world/asia/xinjiang-china-uighurs-prisons.html for one of many articles about the estimated one million Uighurs held in prison camps.

address their priority issues, some of them might be tempted to support a populist dictator who does. Sadly, 46% of American youth don't see democracy as the best form of government[6]!

We are now in the midst of a cold war between democracy and the dictators[7]. Like all wars, this is a complex mess of clashing interests, including economic issues such as access to oil, and territorial control, but at heart the dividing line today is between democratic countries, and dictators. There is little conflict between dictators, who are sanguine about letting each other treat their own people however they wish. The conflicts between democracies are slowly resolved through democratic institutions. When was the last time two democracies went to war with each other? This depends on your definition of war, and of democracy, but a reasonable candidate is the Yugoslavian wars between Serbia, Croatia, and Bosnia which ended in 2001[8], over twenty years ago, a long time in politics.

The conflicts between democracy and dictatorship, however, are more difficult to reconcile. Fundamentally, the dictators wish above all else to cling to power, and so they are threatened by democratic values, which are about regularly changing who has power. Democracies are not inclined to simply leave dictators be, for many reasons, including their autocratic suppression of human rights, and invasions of neighboring democratic allies (for example Russia's invasion of the Ukraine, or China's plan to eventually consume Taiwan).

From Mao's death in 1976 until the ascension of Xi Jinping in 2012, China was in many ways close to converging with the

---

6 For example, see this NBC news article summarizing several polls.

https://www.nbcnews.com/think/opinion/democracy-essential-millennials-increasingly-aren-t-sure-should-concern-us-ncna847476

7 "Is the world entering a new Cold War?" https://www.bbc.com/news/world-us-canada-54244011 -- If the BBC is even asking the question, I suggest it's already a fact.

8 List of wars between democracies: https://en.wikipedia.org/wiki/List_of_wars_between_democracies

democracies. The Party had a regular replacement of leadership every 10 years. Their policies actively grew free markets. They embraced capitalism with its free markets and protection of property rights. They steadily improved their justice system, and accepted some limited but growing free press, freedom of religion, and other personal freedoms. It was common to hear during that phase that you were free in China to do anything except directly criticize the Party. That meant quite a lot of freedom. Yes, Tibetan freedom to protest or worship continued to be suppressed. Yes, China maintained its claim to Taiwan. But China during that long period demonstrably supported "one country two systems", as practiced in Hong Kong, where the Hong Kong government continued years after reunification with China much as before. Taiwan was not vigorously threatened with military invasion, just continually pressured, largely peacefully.

All this has dramatically changed with Xi Jinping. Personal freedoms, which rose after Mao, began to decline again. Censorship has risen. The screws have been steadily tightened on Hong Kong, until in 2019 the city erupted in protest, and in 2020 Beijing passed a law subjugating Hong Kong to mainland security forces. China's military regularly practices for its planned invasion of Taiwan, sending their aircraft carrier, and fighter jets, into Taiwanese territory[9]. Xinjiang province has become a prison state with over a million people in concentration camps[10]. China has reduced the number of

---

9 "Can China invade Taiwan? Here's what could happen if it really does." Business Standard / Bloomberg (Oct 8, 2020). The article presents an even-handed analysis of China's intentions and capabilities. Today, the risk of invasion is relatively low, but it grows steadily. https://www.business-standard.com/article/international/can-china-invade-taiwan-here-s-what-could-happen-if-it-really-does-120100800505_1.html. On March 9, 2021, Admiral Phil Davidson, head of the US Indo-Pacific Command, testified to the Senate that China might invade Taiwan "in this decade, in fact within the next six years."

10 Xinjiang: Large numbers of new detention camps uncovered in report:

American journalists allowed into China[11]. Perhaps most ominously, Xi Jinping has changed the Chinese constitution to prevent the 10-year transition of power which would have had him retire in 2022.

While supported by factual evidence, much of what I write is my personal value judgment, my interpretation of world events, but as many journalists have written, this view is shared by the main strategic planners of both the Democratic and Republican parties in the US. The threat of the new so-called Communism (window dressing for the dictatorship of Xi Jinping) is one of those exceedingly rare things in this world, an agreement of both American parties.

What is the job of the US military? First and foremost, to defend America from invasion[12]. No invasion is currently likely, but the world changes constantly. Today only a handful of organizations have the antipathy and power, such as nuclear weapons or a massive army, to threaten the US[13]: China, North Korea, Russia, and perhaps soon Iran. None of these are particularly motivated to launch such an attack imminently, given the certain and massive consequences. Many organizations have the motivation, but not the means, such as various terrorists who fanatically hate the US.

The second job of the US military is to protect US interests

---

https://www.bbc.com/news/world-asia-china-54277430. Also, see CNN article March 9, 2021: "First independent report into Xinjiang genocide allegations claims evidence of Beijing's 'intent to destroy' Uyghur people"

11 Washington Post, Sep 16, 2020: Western Journalists are getting squeezed out of China by superpower tensions, https://www.washingtonpost.com/lifestyle/media/journalists-get-caught-in-the-middle-of-souring-us-china-relations/2020/09/16/350f8a52-f6ab-11ea-be57-d00bb9bc632d_story.html

12 Or, as stated on the Department of Defense home page, "to deter war and to protect the security of our country". https://archive.defense.gov/about/#mission

13 "These are the biggest threats to the US in 2020", Business Insider (Jan 3, 2020). The article prioritizes them as Russia, Iran, China, North Korea, and ISIS.

worldwide[14]. They are an important tool for the US government to use as appropriate. "US interests" are often very broadly interpreted, too broadly for some. Some Americans, including many Presidents, have included global support of Democracy and other human rights as an American interest, and deployed the military to support them. This was at least one of the reasons, among more selfish ones, for the Vietnam War, the Gulf War, and the operations in Afghanistan.

Is there a significant threat to US interests, however narrowly or broadly defined, requiring a continued 3% of GDP be spent on the military? Should it be higher, or lower? Let's look at that current spending in comparison to the rest of the world, before trying to answer. According to one measure[15], global military spending in 2019 was about 1.9 trillion US dollars. The US was first at $700 billion, and China second at about $200 billion.

I can see why many people think US spending ridiculously high, at over three times as much as China. I would urge them to view the dominant threat not as one country, but as the loose alliance of all the world's dictatorships, which collectively abhor and fear democracy. It is reasonable to plan for the following contingencies, should the dictatorships be left unchecked. I think everything on the following list is a real possibility, within 20 years, if there is no firm opposition backed up by overwhelming military force if needed.

— China plans to absorb Taiwan, which it considers a wayward province.

— China could build sufficient naval presence to effectively control all shipping through the South China Sea. That would be a serious change for over

---

14 According to Military.com, a US military recruiting site: "The military has many missions. Their primary mission of course is to defend the U.S. and U.S. interests." https://www.military.com/join-armed-forces/military-missions-overview.html

15 Stockholm International Peace Research Institute, reported in The Economist of March 27, 2020

20% of world trade[16], through what are currently international waters, conducted freely to international rules, guaranteed by the US Navy. China could choke off a significant fraction of global trade as a pressure tactic to meet whatever interests it chose.

— When powerful enough, China could insist that none of its neighboring countries house US military personnel or equipment, including Korea, Japan, and India. This is what Kennedy insisted during the Cuban Missile Crisis, at least for nuclear weapons, forcing Russia to withdraw from the Caribbean. If China has the military might to do so, I expect they will insist on military domination of their immediate neighborhood.

— Going further, if China has the power, and no equal and opposite power stands against them, they will want effective military control of all their bordering nations, including those across a few hundred miles of ocean. That includes Japan, Korea, and Taiwan. Not coincidentally, that includes 80% of the current global manufacturing capability of advanced semiconductors[17].

— Russia would love to take over the rest of the Ukraine, along with Latvia, Lithuania, and Estonia. Or more.

— Since President Trump abandoned the treaty with Iran which had paused their nuclear weapons program, Iran has worked to develop such weapons as rapidly as they can, toward establishing regional hegemony, meaning that Iran wishes to have control over Iraq

---

16 Over 60% of China's imports pass through the Malacca strait – it is even more important to China than it is to the US. https://chinapower.csis.org/much-trade-transits-south-china-sea/

17 "South Korea and Taiwan's Chip Power Rattles the U.S. and China" https://www.bloomberg.com/news/articles/2021-03-03/chip-shortage-taiwan-south-korea-s-manufacturing-lead-worries-u-s-china

and Afghanistan and other parts of the Middle East, including their oil resources.

Until 2022, this new cold war was largely an arms race with no casualties, and a propaganda war, a public relations contest, much like the conflict of American interests with the Soviet Union of the previous cold war. As I revised this book in 2022, Russia had made it a hot war, invading democratic Ukraine and its 44 million people, killing civilians in massive military strikes. The idea that yet another neighbor country to Russia might stay democratic, and join Europe in its freedom and defense alliance, strikes fear and rage into the dictators in Moscow. Xi Jinping is presumably watching with extreme interest, assessing the democracies' response, wondering what will happen when he similarly invades Taiwan.

I hope and expect that democracy will continue to overwhelmingly win the hearts and minds of most people in every country. Slowly, this will lead to human rights, including the right to vote, spreading worldwide. But the dictators fight back. First, they consolidate their positions, eliminating political opposition within their own countries, building their military forces to prevent overthrow, as much to defend against their own citizens as any foreign invasion[18]. Then they use mixtures of military force and political pressure to win control of "buffer states", namely all countries bordering theirs[19]. So Taiwan is isolated from the United Nations as China bribes or cajoles or pressures other countries to abandon it. So parts of the Ukraine are annexed to Russia. So North Korea is maintained as a prison state with its dictator supported by China's. China's Belt and Road Initiative invests money in 70 countries around the world, with strings attached:

---

18 For example, Venezuela: https://www.aljazeera.com/news/2019/2/23/venezuela-the-military-and-its-support-an-explainer

19 "Russia's Design in The Black Sea: Extending the Buffer Zone"
https://www.csis.org/analysis/russias-design-black-sea-extending-buffer-zone

the initiative consists largely of loans, not grants, with conditions to use Chinese companies, which leaves the recipient countries deeper in debt than they can afford, to China, with infrastructure owned and run by Chinese companies[20].

China's military spending is rising at about 10% per year, at around 2% of their GDP. Today they are not a threat to the US, in terms of all-out war, but close to home, the balance tilts. American ability to protect Taiwan, South Korea, Japan, and other allies, close to China's shores, is eroding fast. Already Pentagon analysts believe US aircraft carriers would be vulnerable to Chinese missiles, if brought close enough to defend any of those countries from Chinese action[21].

How can we reduce the risks of dictatorships expanding to more countries, and keep at least the majority of the world's economy, with all the power that entails, in the hands of governments that support human rights?

1. The US should continue spending 3% of GDP on its military, to remain the overwhelming leader, until the entire world has democratic governments supporting human rights. This is a cost worth paying, at the very least to retain those rights for Americans. Less is not an option – in fact at current rates the Pentagon is frequently losing its strategic war games with China.[22]

20 For example, "in some markets Chinese investment has nearly become a euphemism for wasteful spending, environmental destruction and untenable debt." Forbes, January 2020.
https://www.forbes.com/sites/wadeshepard/2020/01/29/how-chinas-belt-and-road-became-a-global-trail-of-trouble/?sh=6f770480443d

21 "Chinese Threats to U.S. Surface Ships", The RAND Corporation. Key finding: "China has rapidly improved its ability to reliably locate and to attack U.S. carrier-strike groups at distances of up to 2,000 km from its coast." https://www.rand.org/pubs/research_briefs/RB9858z4.html

22 See "'We're going to lose fast': US Air Force held a war game that started with a Chinese biological attack." In Yahoo! News, March 10, 2021. Read the interview with Lt. General Clinton Hinote, deputy chief of staff for strategy.

Why 3%? Why not 2.5%, or 2.0%, or 5%? I believe maintaining at 3% sends a strong message to both our allies and potential enemies. I hope that with appropriate focus, the Pentagon can overcome its strategic weaknesses vis a vis China, given the balance of spending. To the extent China and other dictatorships become more democratic and supportive of human rights, the 3% should drop. To the extent that China's strategic threats described in this chapter grow, I think at some point an even higher expenditure might be necessary. Deterrence is much, much cheaper than war[23].

2. The US should build stronger mutual defense relationships with all its democratic allies around the world, to balance the growing capability of the dictatorships. NATO is a logical starting point. The US should sponsor growth of NATO to include all democracies around the world, with priority to those crucial to the global economy, such as Taiwan, Korea, and Japan. This means clearly and strongly saying "no" to any dictatorship trying to invade any democracy. Such a global defense organization would be large and strong enough that no dictatorship could ever prevail to take away human rights in the democratic countries. For America itself, which often has an isolationist bent, this strength through alliance would guarantee America's own freedom, to an extent that America alone could not. Imagine the other extreme, if America withdrew to its own devices, and Russia slowly took over all of Europe, while China took over all of Asia.

---

23 Perhaps "deterrence is cheaper than war" is obvious, but for those who wish quantitative, evidence-based reasoning, here is an article analyzing the balance for a particularly important case:

https://www.realcleardefense.com/articles/2016/10/13/the_economics_of_conventional_deterrence_in_europe_110203.html

At that point, even the US military would not be enough, with the entire rest of the world against it.

3. In exchange for US involvement in that alliance, every country must commit to spending at least 2% of their GDP on defense, with strong treaty penalties such as tariffs and fines, for those who do not spend the 2%, until such time as the entire world is democratic. This commitment is theoretically already there for NATO, but not honored[24]. I support strong action to achieve that reasonable threshold, including increased political and economic pressure on those democratic allies until they meet their commitment. The awakening due to Russia's invasion of the Ukraine has already helped, as did Trump's vocal pressures on the deadbeats.

4. Within the military budget, there must be a priority placed on technology research, to stay ahead of the military technology of dictatorships, particularly China.

5. Although military strength is required, in a world threatened by dictatorships, military action should be the last resort. I put the non-military actions later in this list, but they are equally important. Nonmilitary actions will be more effective to win those hearts and minds. Every dictatorship will eventually fall, if nearly everyone wants democracy. Democracy must be defended by making it desirable. This means winning lots of other battles: making the US health care system the best in the world, keeping our freedom of the press and freedom of speech, continuing support for the best university system in the world, and a vibrant democracy where everyone feels hope for an always better world.

---

24 "Defence Expenditure of NATO Countries (2013-2020)", from NATO's website (Oct 21, 2020) https://www.nato.int/cps/en/natohq/news_178975.htm

6. We might win the Cold War with China the same way Reagan won the Cold War with the Soviets: he negotiated nuclear arms treaties with them, kept communications open, but invested heavily in military strength as well as making America strong economically. The Soviet empire collapsed from the financial strain of trying to keep up. That may be harder to achieve with China, but is one possible path. Even better to negotiate constantly, finding ways to live with each other peaceably, finding as many ways as possible to develop mutual trust, to avoid military conflict, to be very clear on the exact lines which would cause military conflict, so that neither will ever cross them.

While I believe these are sufficient reasons to keep spending so much of our GDP on the military, there are additional spin-off benefits of keeping it strong. Military research spins off commercial products. Military careers give young people options to learn, including technical skills, travel, discipline, and values of service and teamwork. The military can provide special services during national emergencies, such as transportation, engineering, and protection. In some future utopia, when military forces are no longer needed, these could come from other organizations, but for now they are a side benefit of having a strong Pentagon.

This need is not forever. I am optimistic that the human rights I began this chapter with will grow worldwide, and eventually the entire Earth will be democratic. Then military spending can fade to zero, and we can spend that 3% of GDP on other priorities. Even the greatest threat to world peace, that is the increasing aggression of China's dictatorship, has a ticking timeout clock – China's population is shrinking instead of growing, and its GDP growth is not what it used to be. Given the increasingly repressive government interfering in the economy, and prioritizing government control over Chinese quality of life, Xi Jinping's ability to continue growing his military strength will be increasingly limited.

3: OIL AND COAL

My daughter was born on April 22, 1995. I already had three boys, and was of course extremely happy to finally have a girl. I was actually hoping she'd hang on a little longer, and share a birthday with Shakespeare, but it wasn't to be. She was born instead on Earth Day. That was the 25th Earth Day celebrated. The year I first wrote this chapter, she turned 25 while Earth Day turned 50. I remember when she was born scientists already worried deeply about global warming. They are far more concerned today, though not all Americans agree.

If you don't believe in global warming, or perhaps don't think the US needs to do anything about it, you might skip the first half of this chapter, which won't convince you differently, and read my action plan. What I propose doing will make America stronger not weaker, richer not poorer, and is designed to appeal as much to free market small government Republicans as it should to environment-warrior Democrats.

Despite official Republican disregard in the US, climate change is the number one political issue on our planet, as measured by the World Economic Forum's annual poll[25] at least three years in a row. Global warming hasn't directly affected some of us yet. You may or may not believe Hurricane Katrina would have hit New Orleans without it, but Category 4 and 5 hurricanes have doubled since 1990[26].

As a scientist, I was convinced pretty early that global warming is real, and that it is extremely dangerous for humanity. I may not convince doubters with the following stories, but the actions I list in this chapter to deal with climate change will not bankrupt our government, nor destroy our industrial leadership of the world, but in fact do the opposite — so even if you don't think global warming is a problem, you might like the actions I recommend. Even though the US is no longer the biggest carbon emitter, which is China, with India as #3 growing fast, and the US at #2[27], America has a unique chance to benefit from the global transformation, because of its technological capability and wealth.

Whether global warming is real or not, here are a few of the people and groups of people who believe it is real and dangerous:

1. **The Pentagon**, which reported to Congress in 2019 that climate change poses significant threat to two

25 Number one by impact, number two by likelihood https://reports.weforum.org/global-risks-report-2020/a-decade-

left/#:~:text=Indeed%2C%20%E2%80%9Cfailure%20of%20climate%2D,likelihood%2C%20accordin g%20to%20survey%20respondents.

26 According the National Science Foundation, "Number of Category 4 and 5 Hurricanes Has Doubled Over the Past 35 Years"

https://www.nsf.gov/news/news_summ.jsp?cntn_id=104428#:~:text=Since%201990%2C%20the%20 number%20of,of%20156%20mph%20or%20more.

27 "Each Country's Share of CO2 Emissions" updated Aug 12, 2020
https://www.ucsusa.org/resources/each-countrys-share-co2-emissions

thirds of mission-essential military installations in the US, and has an ongoing multi-million dollar program to review and mitigate the challenges of floods, drought, storms, and other impacts[28].

2.   **The voters of Wisconsin, our ultimate purple state.** Wisconsin is arguably the most purple state in the Union today. Trump won it by about 23,000 votes in 2016 and lost by about 20,000 in 2020. As I write this, we have a Democrat governor and Republican legislature. And yet a solid majority of 62% believe climate change is a problem warranting active government policies[29].

3.   In February 2021 Yale University in conjunction with FaceBook interviewed 76,328 people in 31 countries about their opinions on climate change. The country least concerned about it was Nigeria, but even there 58% of people were "worried" or "very worried". Asked whether it should be a government priority for action, support ranged from 55% in Egypt to 91% in Mexico.

4.   The governments of 187 countries who have ratified the Paris Agreement on climate change, most of whom have taken actions, whether sufficient or not. From the same Yale study mentioned above, 74% of Americans support the Paris Agreement.

5.   78% of the millennial generation worldwide, who say they are willing to change their lifestyle to protect the environment.[30]

---

28 "The effects of a changing climate are a national security issue"

https://climateandsecurity.org/2019/01/new-pentagon-report-the-effects-of-a-changing-climate-are-a-national-security-issue/

29 Milwaukee Journal Sentinel, Aug 29, 2022. The poll reported 65% of voters country-wide felt the same. Ironically, the poll showed people on average think only 43% of other people agree with them. The majority doesn't realize it's a majority.

30 https://www.businessinsider.com/world-problems-most-serious-according-to-millennials-2017-8

6. **97% of climate scientists (according to NASA)**[31], with official statements from 18 US and international scientific societies, who through thousands of forums and petitions and papers have tried to warn us over the past several decades. 50 years ago, it was a fraction of scientists with unproven theories. Over time, the evidence has mounted, and counter-claims have been disproven. There do remain climate skeptics including tenured professors and well-known scientists, but they are a tiny if vocal minority.

Let's assume for the moment the majority is correct in this case, and the primary cause of a dangerous rise in global temperatures is carbon-based gases humans are adding to the atmosphere. Those models predict that even if we stopped now, there is enough to keep us warming dangerously for decades. At our current rate of pumping, the impact to global lifestyles and economies will be massive, such as turning large fractions of the Earth into deserts, including much of the United States, doubling the number of Category 5 hurricanes from today's already high level, melting the rest of both poles and all of Greenland, raising sea levels so a third of the planet's population is flooded.

Some of my left-wing friends are despondent. They think it is too late, that the oil industry has won, and that humanity is doomed. I believe they are too pessimistic. Here is some good news. Solar and wind power, including all the manufacturing and setup costs, are cheaper today than coal or natural gas. Not in northern climates for solar, of course, and not in calm climates for wind, but on average around the world, yes. This is why the majority of new energy plants worldwide are now "green." Republican Texas generates more electricity from wind than coal, as of 2019, and its solar energy capacity is doubling every year. Solar power is now the

---

[31] https://climate.nasa.gov/scientific-consensus/

cheapest energy on Earth[32], despite government subsidies to the oil and coal industries of 5 trillion dollars per year[33]. On May 28, 2020, the Wall Street Journal reported the Energy Information Administration's data, that the US is now using more renewable energy than coal, for the first time since 1885. There is no going back. Some estimates say we need a carbon price of $100 per ton of CO2 to achieve the Paris objectives, which would raise the price of gasoline in the US by a bit less than $1 a gallon[34]. That's steep, as we experienced with the inflation burst of 2022, but may not be necessary, given the change in energy economics already.

Why does anyone still build a power plant using coal or gas? Government subsidies. Various governments around the world are trying to maintain jobs for people in the coal or gas industry, and they sponsor such plants. China's national government, for example, afraid of backlash against coal pollution at home, increasingly built coal-fired power plants around the world rather than at home, as part of its "aid" packages, employing their engineers and supporting their coal industry[35]. And local governments in China have been building about one coal plant a week to support their local coal industry, even though the cost is higher than solar, and even though the Chinese federal government is against it. Perhaps there is a role

[32] https://www.carbonbrief.org/solar-is-now-cheapest-electricity-in-history-confirms-iea

[33] https://www.imf.org/en/Publications/WP/Issues/2019/05/02/Global-Fossil-Fuel-Subsidies-Remain-Large-An-Update-Based-on-Country-Level-Estimates-46509

[34] Unsettled, by Steve Koonin, an oil company researcher who denies most of climate change, did the math to estimate 35 c/gallon for a $40 price, so I assume it's no worse than this.

[35] "Squeezing out the carbon" in The Economist, Sep 3, 2021. I noted China "built" rather than "builds" coal plants through its Belt & Road Initiatives. With the price of solar and wind now beating coal, China spent $0 on coal plants in the first half of 2021, after canceling $47 billion of them in 2019-2020.

for government to create jobs for people, but I prefer leaving job creation to the free market. I'd suggest that money go elsewhere. Let's take 100% of the money currently subsidizing carbon industries, and give it back to the citizens who need it, in more constructive ways. More on that later.

Unfortunately, the number of existing power plants and vehicles and other things pumping carbon into the atmosphere remain too voluminous, and market economics will take too long to transform the global economy to carbon-free, or even carbon-reduced energy sufficient to stop a disastrous level of warming.

Fortunately, there is an answer. The Pinatubo eruption of 1991 cooled the Earth by about half a degree for 4 years[36]. When I read this, I was filled with hope. Simply dumping a few tons of volcanic ash into the atmosphere can undo 25% of global warming, hitting the pause button for several years! It is not a long term answer to the amount of carbon cooking us now, but it can delay the crisis and give us time to find a permanent answer.

For one of my favorite summer vacations ever, we rented a Cruise America RV in San Francisco, and drove a long loop through six national parks: Yosemite, Death Valley, Bryce Canyon, Zion, Grand Canyon, and Joshua Tree. As we drove into Death Valley one morning, we had the A/C running at max and were still getting a little too warm. We pulled over to see some shifting sand dunes and eat lunch. It was so hot, we couldn't walk outside more than a few minutes. I had to run the generator to max the A/C while we ate lunch, and it was still pretty hot. It occurred to me that if our A/C failed and we couldn't get out fast, we could die. It was a bit scary. With global warming at its current stage, it's like we're driving the world into Death Valley at about 9am. It isn't horrifically hot yet, but we know it's getting hotter and hotter. We may not want to turn on the global A/C yet, but it's not an option to

[36] The Economist Mar 14, 2019.

do without it.

Global warming was not caused by America alone, and in fact the biggest threat today comes from China, India, and Brazil. America's carbon emissions have already been dropping for years. But saving the world from cataclysmic warming requires bold technological leadership. I'd like America to lead the solution to global warming. Given how much carbon has already been pumped into the atmosphere, and how hard it will be to stop, we need dramatic high tech action on three fronts: shifting to carbon-free energy, countering global warming with global cooling, and removing carbon from the atmosphere.

With concerted global effort, we can shift to largely carbon-free energy within a few decades. Solar and wind energy are already cheaper than coal. Electric vehicles are close to the same cost as gasoline chuggers. I would prefer government stay out of the decision-making about how to get carbon-free, and let the market decide. Government's role can be very simple: steadily remove the tax policies which currently subsidize carbon, stop oil and gas and coal subsidies, and add a tiny and very slowly growing carbon tax. These measures will inevitably push all industries to shift steadily to non-carbon energy. Keeping the carbon tax very small to begin with will prevent sudden dislocations to companies and people, but a published schedule to slowly raise it over time will allow everyone to make profitable decisions about shifting. Since sustainable energy is already cheaper than carbon, the carbon tax can be very small, primarily symbolic to start, to support the transformation.

Globally governments subsidize carbon-base1d energy to the tune of $5.9 trillion[37]. The US can phase out its subsidies

---

[37]

https://www.imf.org/en/Publications/WP/Issues/2021/09/23/Still-Not-Getting-Energy-Prices-Right-A-Global-and-Country-Update-of-Fossil-Fuel-Subsidies-466004 over several years, and give the tax savings back to Americans to use on the energy of their choice. The US can motivate other countries to do the same, through moral leadership, and financial incentives – for example charging a carbon tax on any country's exports to the US, at the same level as that country's carbon subsidies.

The second necessary change is global cooling, since global warming has built up too much momentum already. This is turning on the A/C in Death Valley. Some environmentalists seriously propose that we need to shrink the human population, or shrink GDP (that is, to reduce the standard of living for people rather than increase it) to save the world. To me, that's like sawing off your leg below the knee to get out of a bear trap, when there's a wrench sitting right beside you to pry open the trap. Government should sponsor more research into methods to cool the planet and decarbonize the atmosphere, as industry has little direct motivation to do so. Perhaps replanting forests worldwide would be sufficient. Perhaps more technological solutions are needed. America's scientists and innovative companies can figure out the optimal way. By contrast, the US spent $28 million on energy storage technology last year, while offering coal companies $150 million in subsidies, part of the US carbon subsidies that Forbes Magazine (June 15, 2019) estimated at $649 billion per year.

Climate Engineering scares many people, and may indeed be dangerous, but we are already beyond the point where we can do without it[38]. Opening a bear trap that has your ankle in its jaws is dangerous, as you might start bleeding profusely… so do you just leave the trap on your leg and live with it? The consequences of flooding, rising sea levels, more powerful storms, and other global warming effects are upon us, and

---

38 "Floating a trial balloon: a controversial climate experiment could soon begin in Sweden" (The Economist, Feb 27, 2021). This article talks about current climate engineering research, its opposition, and its possible necessity for keeping global temperature rises below a cataclysmic 1.5 degrees.

likely worse than a measured program of global cooling. I'd sponsor an active research program which includes cloud-seeding, and other forms of "heat mirrors" to directly counter global warming. As we learn more about the science and engineering, we can ramp up those efforts as needed to balance the carbon we have already put in the atmosphere, and the carbon we continue to upload for the coming decades, until we have completely shifted to carbon-free energy, and pulled enough carbon out of the sky.

Coal and oil were a fantastic energy revolution and a big part of what made America a superpower, but now they are the horse and buggy. Do we want to cede the next energy revolution to China, who already dominates the solar power industry? Or will America again be the world leader in the next energy revolution?

4: HEALTH CARE

I met a young woman in Milwaukee who suffered occasional terribly painful seizures. Months earlier, she had been to a doctor about them, and diagnosed with lupus. It's a relatively rare disease, works a bit like AIDS, but more episodic, and of unknown cause. I knew a little about what she was dealing with, because I had another friend in Vancouver suffering from the same disease. The Vancouver friend had excellent medical care, the same comprehensive health care enjoyed by all Canadians, so I knew there was treatment available. But my Milwaukee friend was not getting any treatment at all. Her doctor told her she might die without it, but she couldn't afford it. She was excited to have just got a job – but that job came without health benefits, and because she was working, she had just lost access to Medicaid. While researching this updated edition of Hope, I reached out to ask if she could have afforded one of the new subsidized marketplace packages, given her low income, but I never heard back from her. I don't know if she made it.

The US spends about twice as much per person on health care as most other countries on Earth[39], but gets worse results, for the average person, than any other advanced economy. It is the best of states, and the worst of states. If you want the best care in the world, and can afford it, come to the US. It has the best hospitals, best treatments, best technology, best doctors, best nurses, best drugs, and best science. It also has worse results, on average for its citizens, than most other OECD countries:

- 11th place for infant mortality, behind China, for example, and Turkey. World Atlas ranks 54 countries as doing better than the US on this metric.[40]
- Along with Venezuela and Syria, one of the handful of countries on Earth where maternal mortality actually rose in the last 20 years.
- 7th place for overall health. Canada, with universal health care costing half as much as the US spends per person, is in 1st place.
- The only country in the OECD without universal coverage (check The Atlantic's 2012 article with a map of countries that don't have universal coverage — the US keeps company with Venezuela, Turkey, Albania, China, and Iran).
- 28th place by overall longevity.
- 20,000 Americans die every year due to lack of health care[41].

To be first in spending, and get such terrible results for it,

---

39 The Healing of America, by T.R. Reid, 2009. See his investigation comparing US health care with Germany, France, Britain, Canada, Japan, India, and others. It starts with a story of lupus killing an American, a weird coincidence for me as I'd written the intro to this chapter before reading his book. More recent data puts the US at 17% of GDP on health care, while most rich countries spend about 11%, so it's not "double" for America's peer group... but 50% higher is bad enough.

40 Infant Mortality Rate by Country, in World Atlas.com

41 Also from "The Healing of America", by T.R. Reid.

is an unconscionable shame and waste of taxpayer money. Yes taxpayer money, since the US has one of the most socialized medical systems in the world, for 40% of its people, that is the ones on government programs. If we spent twice as much per person on Olympic sports performance, and placed 7th in the world, we would have bipartisan support for a scientific program to improve, and we'd boost ourselves to first place within ten years. We put a man on the Moon in ten years. We can fix health care.

It's not hopeless. We could make the US the best health care country in the world, while making it less socialist instead of more, less expensive instead of more, and boosting our economy through greater health. Let's not use the Canadian system, which in my frank opinion is probably the second worst in the rich world, after the US. Let's take the best system in the world, and improve on it, to make the US #1. Which country has that? Google, or read on.

Personally, I've felt guilty at the fantastic care I've received since moving to the US. I have a great career, always covered by excellent health insurance plans. On moving to Milwaukee from Vancouver, Canada, my care actually improved. I got an MRI in a week, when I needed one, while in Canada I was put on a waiting list that took several months. Here in the US I see a specialist within a couple weeks if I want to, while in Canada I waited three to six months. But health care has cost me about $10,000 per year here, for my partner plus myself, in addition to what our employers paid into our plans. I am fortunate that I can afford this. It's a stretch for most Americans, and impossible for millions of them. All other rich countries have steadily increasing life expectancy, while the US has actually seen a decline in several demographics, even before Covid-19.

How can we retain the best of American care, the world's best for those who can pay, while taking decent care of every citizen?

Here's one radical view: the problem is already solved. The Affordable Care Act has flourished despite several attempts to kill it. Its price cap of 8.5% of income puts affordable health care within reach of all Americans. Sure, we still pay double for a worse product, on average, but at least everyone can buy it.

For me, this isn't good enough, so I will take a few pages to describe a radical proposal to improve our system.

I gained a fascinating insight from T R Reid's "Healing of America" – that US health care is really a mix of different systems from around the world.

One large part of America lives under a totally socialist model, similar to the UK, where the government runs and pays for and provides 100% of the health care: the military's TriCare, the VA.

Another big part of American health care, about 20% of it, and the most popular, was designed to copy the Canadian system, where the government negotiates and pays for health care, but the hospitals and doctors and other providers are private. They named it after the Canadian system: Medicare.

But the biggest part of American health care is based on the German system invented by Baron Otto von Bismark, where thousands of insurance companies negotiate with private providers, and offer comprehensive insurance to all employees. The primary differences are that in Germany, the insurance companies are all nonprofit, and 100% of Germans get coverage, subsidized by government for those who don't have an employer to do so.

Then there are the uninsured and under-insured, who "pay as they go" for as much or little health care as they can afford, just like the poorest African countries.

My favorite approach for the US would be a brand new made-in-America system, using less government and more innovation. I would make health care like car insurance. The government does not sell anyone car insurance. The government does not provide free car insurance to poor people. Instead, the government creates a competitive market by enforcing that every car on the road must have a certain minimum insurance policy attached. Similarly, every American should have a certain minimum health insurance, compatible with America being one of the richest countries on Earth.

Richer people should be free to upgrade their health care as much as they like, but the minimum plan should be decent.

Medicare and Medicaid and the VA could all be converted to nonprofits outside the government, retaining all their staff and standards and processes, and providing the same service they do today. The minimum health care should be at least as good as the standards for these, and most employer-sponsored plans today. With the privatizing of Medicare and Medicaid, this, already partly done via Medicare Advantage, would mean a dramatic increase in the market available to competitive companies. With the regulation of minimum plans, and preventing any company from refusing any citizen, as well as regulations to govern what conditions may allow higher or lower premiums, all citizens could get affordable health care. This would dramatically improve the average health, longevity, and productivity of the American people.

Not all Americans could afford the premiums this would lead to. Here's how we could handle that. Anyone who does not of themselves purchase a Health Care Plan, will get the cheapest one available in their state, bought for them by the federal government, the cost added to their taxes. This is not a fine, just a basic tax to ensure a minimum standard, similar to current Social Security and Medicare taxes, and in fact replacing the latter.

How do we handle the financing of all these continuing programs, since so many of them currently depend on government taxes? For example, Medicare beneficiaries pay on average $5460 per year out of pocket for their healthcare as of 2016 out of a total of approximately $14,000 spending[42], with taxes paying the rest. Would beneficiaries have to pay the full $14,000? No. I propose the government stop paying the new nonprofits, but take the same money, and return it to all those

---

[42] https://www.medicareresources.org/faqs/how-much-does-the-average-medicare-beneficiary-pay-out-of-pocket-for-medical-expenses/

beneficiaries, plus the uninsured.

Let's have a look at how that would affect various Americans. Start with the average Medicare user. Today their total health care cost is about $14,000. If they have average income, they're paying about $5460 per year in premiums and deductibles and co-pays. If they have higher than average income, they're paying more. If they have very low income, they are paying close to zero, with Medicaid kicking in. Under the new system, without any socialism, the premiums will be just over $1000/month to cover the full cost – but they'll get about $8540/year ($14000 - $5460) in lower taxes. That's in the first year, if we don't have any cost savings. But with all the health insurance companies actually competing with each other for a change, the cost will come down. There is waste in all that government bureaucracy.

Let's look at another sample American. Let's take an employee who makes above-average wages working for a large company. She pays 1.45% of her wages as Medicare tax, as well as other income taxes the federal government uses to pay current Medicare, Medicaid, Military, and VA health care. Practically none of that 1.45% is saved up by the government to pay her future Medicare bills; the money goes out as it comes in. She pays a widely varying amount in premiums and co-pays and deductibles and out-of-pocket expenses, depending on her health. What she pays directly can vary from a few $100 to about $10,000 per year, even with an employer plan. (I speak from experience.) Her company pays another 1.45% toward Medicare, and also pays about $6000 per year for her health insurance plan[43], and also pays federal taxes on their profit, which goes to other health subsidies. If she's "average" she pays about $500 per month out of pocket. What happens to her under the new system? That depends on free market decisions her employer and their health insurance company make. The taxes will not change, but the insurance company will be required to offer that same plan to everyone in the US, at no higher rate than they charge her and her company. Will their rates go up or down? What do you think would happen to health insurance rates, if all the insurance companies actually had to compete with each other for all Americans' business, and offer the same minimum product? Today American health care has the highest administration costs in the world, the highest direct cost, the highest prescription drug costs, the highest health care profits, and about the worst average health care in the rich world. I think some competition, as there is in most European countries with better health care than the US, would help not hurt.

Government would define what a minimum Health Care Plan has to cover, with rules to prevent companies from refusing coverage, or cherry-picking healthy citizens. Companies would be free to innovate on additional coverage, and how to manage provision. Government would stay out. Government would get out of health care provision entirely, privatize all VA hospitals, move the entire Medicare and Medicaid bureaucracy into non-profit insurance companies. The free market, with federal rules for fairness, would constantly compete to provide the best health care in the world, and every American would be covered to a good minimum standard.

All the federal government would do, in the spirit of small government, is establish a minimal set of rules, and a system to enforce them. This would be far smaller than the current massive bureaucracies of overlapping government medical programs. Establish the minimum standard of coverage, and require every company that offers health insurance in a given state to offer that minimum plan, to offer it to everyone in the state, and that it be their lowest cost plan. No refusing anybody. No refusing any claim under the standard policy. That ensures no American citizen gets less than the standard.

And it does it while decreasing government spending rather than increasing it.

I would expect this greater role for the free market to motivate huge amounts of creativity, to provide better health care for less money, as competitors vie for those health care dollars. More choice leads to more competition, which leads to better service.

If the private sector insurance companies are unable to provide the same service on the standard policy as the new non-profit Medicare and Medicaid organizations, then they will have to change. Take less profit, become more efficient, change their processes. Since all insurance companies will have to offer the same standard policy, they'll all have to compete on their internal efficiencies, and win customers. Since Medicare is currently far more efficient in terms of administrative overhead than most private insurers, and doesn't make a profit, I expect a large fraction of Americans would use the Medicare offering, until private insurers up their game.

What would this achieve, financially? It would remove socialism from American health care. It would reduce administrative costs, which in America are around 15% higher than other countries – enough to fully insure everyone in America who isn't yet, and still have savings left over[44].

At least two major challenges remain, even if you like the ideas above. One is how to make it happen politically, and another is how to implement it over time without creating transition chaos or economic crisis.

On the political front, I'm encouraged by the story of Taiwan's transformation in the 1990s. The conservative government was concerned about losing an election, as the liberals were pushing a platform of universal health care. The election looked close, so the conservatives pulled a sneaky

---

44 Health Care Administrative Costs in the United States and Canada, 2017, by Himmelstein, Campbell, and Woolhandlr, in the Annals of Internal Medicine, January 21, 2020

trick: they stole the liberals' platform, and promised health care reform. They won, hired an American consultant, looked at all the best health care systems in the world, and implemented one of them. I wonder if the same could happen in the US? Rather than the progressive wing of the Democrats trying to get a heavily socialist scheme past a Republican filibuster, why not a Republican health care reform based on free market principles? In fact, the plan I put forward in this chapter is more free-market than the current mix of systems in the US, and should appeal to conservatives – while still achieving the economic boost of health care for all.

How do we implement a very different health care system without causing painful economic disruption during the transition? If we save billions of dollars getting rid of administrative bloat, to spend on health care for the under-insured, won't that mean millions of layoffs? Even if it means more jobs for doctors and nurses, doesn't it mean less jobs for insurance office workers?

There is a way. First, it's useful to consider that every other developed country has done this transformation already, somewhere in the past hundred years, and many of them within a brief period of a few years, like Taiwan. We can learn from them.

Part of an effective transition would be to not change too much all at once, to keep most elements of the current system in place for a period of time. Keep the Medicare and Medicaid and VA organizations, keep all the HMOs and health insurance companies. Phase in the new rules over several years. The key rules will themselves transform the organizations, to adapt and survive in the new market:

1. Define the new American Standard for Health Insurance. This would not be a brand new document. It could start simply with Medicare. Over the years, it could be refined to add or subtract things.

2. Every organization that offers health insurance would have to offer their package to every American who wants it, in stages over a few years. By the end of the

few years, no refusing anyone, for any reason. You can offer better plans for more money, but your cheapest plan must meet the national standard and be available for anyone in the US to buy.

3. Require everyone receiving income from the government to have health insurance, so that welfare or whatever other payments they get from government go first to health care, and then to other needs.

What impact would this have? Would it really hurt the giant health insurance company of a Fortune 500 client to be forced to offer their plan for the same price to everyone in the US? Would they have to raise their rates, to offer the same level of service as Medicare? The biggest difference would be getting the remaining millions of Americans who are currently uninsured or under-insured, to have similar health care to all their compatriots. That does not come free, but at least they will get the same deal as the richer half, instead of higher rates than the rich pay. The uninsured tend to be relatively poor, so the only way this can get paid for is increased government support, along with prioritizing health care in those support dollars. Today, huge amounts of government money subsidize the health care costs of the richer half, while spending zero on the uninsured. That should shift, so the rich pay somewhat more for their health care, and nobody goes without. That's in the short run. In the longer run, a free market system for American health care (unlike the heavily subsidized and socialist and oligopololistic systems in the US today), will make the system more efficient. Don't think the math adds up? Canada gets better health results at 50% lower cost than the US. Don't you think that with competition, US health care could shave 10% off its costs and use that to fill the 10% gap so no American is left behind?

This is more or less how France implemented their health care system decades ago. They have many insurance companies. If you're French, you can choose any one of them, and pay the sliding scale premiums depending on your income, something like the Medicare tax in the US. The coverage rules and costs for each service are set by government, negotiated with providers. The providers are all private companies – doctors, hospitals, clinics. It's less socialist than the US, except the insurance companies can't refuse any patient, nor can they refuse any legitimate claim from any health provider in the country.

When the World Health Organization[45] ranked all the health care systems in the world, they called France #1. The US ranked #37, in between Costa Rica and Slovenia. Let's beat France. Let's do it in less than ten years.

---

45 World Health Report, 2000, by the World Health Organization. The report still gets a lot of media attention 20 years later, ranking France as #1 in the word, the US as #37.

5: THE RIGHT TO BEAR ARMS

"*A well regulated militia being necessary to the security of a free state, the right of the people to keep and bear arms shall not be infringed.*" So says the Second Amendment to the Constitution of the United States, as ratified by Thomas Jefferson.

Gun rights are a uniquely American issue, similar to the abortion debate. In both cases the rest of the civilized world has gone through public debates, violent disagreements, slowly evolving opinions, and finally a consensus, accepted by all major parties. In the US, the debates still rage, a significant factor in political contests. Like so many other issues in America, polarization has put Republicans and Democrats on opposite sides. Republicans usually support the NRA in fighting any gun control. Democrats, despite 65% of Americans wanting increased gun control, have failed to make much legislative progress after decades of mass shootings of children. After the Uvalde elementary school massacre, a handful of Republicans did join to sign some very limited gun control in 2022, the first significant change in 20 years.

In August 2019 Fox News did a poll, finding two thirds of Americans favor a ban on assault weapons and semi-automatics. The majority may have no idea what defines an assault weapon, or what distinguishes automatic from semi-automatic, but they believe gun control should be higher, not lower. In 2019, there was on average more than one mass shooting per day in America, a mass shooting defined as four or more deaths. And yet those two thirds of Americans (according to Fox News) are ignored by their Congress.

Antonin Scalia, intellectual leader of the conservatives on the Supreme Court, wrote "Like most rights, the Second Amendment right is not unlimited. It is not a right to keep and carry any weapon whatsoever in any manner whatsoever and for whatever purpose." Yes, perhaps the most famous conservative justice actually said there can be limits to the right to bear arms.

But what limits should society levy? I don't want to take away the right to own a gun. I am a huge fan of personal freedom. I think most Americans should be able to buy a gun, or a hundred guns, including a fully automatic assault weapon, if they want to, and not have government get in the way, for example by charging massive fees, or requiring massive amounts of paperwork. That said, I agree with Scalia, and think there should be some reasonable limitations, more than are currently in place.

To drive a car in America, you have to pass a driving test and obtain a driving license. If you want to drive taxis or large commercial trucks or motorcycles, you need to pass a more specialized test, and maintain a more difficult license. How about the same structure for guns, which kill about the same number of Americans as cars do? Almost nobody complains that driver licensing rules obstruct our freedom to own a car.

There are several areas where American rights to life, liberty, and the pursuit of happiness are systematically abrogated. Let's start with the right to life. Huge numbers of deaths are at least theoretically preventable, such as those from hospital errors, smoking, obesity, alcohol, sexually transmitted diseases, and treatable cancers. Most of these are largely up to personal choices, and I would prefer government stay out of people's freedom. Yes, some research and public education can be done to reduce these deaths, and there should be some spending, but not as a top government priority. On the other hand, there are two major types of death which are often one person causing the death of another: firearms (39,000 per year), and car accidents (43,000 per year). The latter shrinks every year as cars get safer, and will get close to zero with self-driving cars; government can in due course help that by mandating self-driving cars, similar to the mandate that people wear seat belts.

The US is the only advanced country where firearms kill more than 10 people per 100,000 every year[46], with about 4 times as many firearm deaths per person as second-place Finland, among "first or second world" countries. The US is at a low extreme on the spectrum of regulation. I support the right of Americans to own guns, just as Americans should be allowed to buy as many cars as they like, but subject to regulations to protect the lives of their fellow Americans. I urge America to require extensive training and licensing to own assault weapons, and require background checks to prevent violent ex-cons and psychologically challenged people from having guns. I like the comparison with cars. Nobody doubts that Americans can buy as many cars as they like and can afford. But in the interests of killing fewer people, there are safety regulations on cars, and licensing requirements, and rules about where and how you can drive.

I have tried to understand the viewpoint of American conservatives who don't want increased gun control. (Recall,

---

[46] https://www.worldatlas.com/articles/countries-with-the-highest-rates-of-firearm-related-deaths.html#:~:text=Countries%20With%20The%20Highest%20Rates%20Of%20Firearm%20Related,%20%2034.1%20%2016%20more%20rows%20

about 65% of Americans want more control, which must include some conservatives.) About 10% of Americans want even less control, and the remaining 25% feel the current level is about right. So what do those 35% who don't want any more gun control believe? I group their statements, as I've heard them, into the following categories:

1.   Guns aren't the problem, so controlling guns won't help.
2.   Most of those deaths are criminals killing criminals.
3.   Most of those deaths are suicides.
4.   Don't worry: as white middle class, your chances of getting shot are very low, since it's mostly black people getting shot.
5.   The Constitution says we have the right to own guns. The Democrats are trying to take away our rights to even own hunting rifles.
6.   If everybody had a gun, criminals would not be able to murder so easily. The solution to the number of gun deaths in America is more guns.
7.   The guns used in murders are mostly illegal, so gun control legislation won't decrease the murder rate.

Let's discuss each of these in turn. First, will reducing the number or type of guns on the legal market do any good, if the reason for deaths is not guns themselves, but the underlying intent of the people firing them? Statistically, around the world, where there are far fewer guns, there are fewer gun deaths[47]. Guns are a top-ten cause of death in the US, but not in any other advanced country, where guns face various degrees of

---

[47]

https://www.npr.org/sections/goatsandsoda/2021/03/24/9808 38151/gun-violence-deaths-how-the-u-s-compares-to-the-rest-of-the-world#:~:text=The%20U.S.%20has%20the%2032nd-highest%20rate%20of%20deaths,United%20Kingdom%2C%20w hich%20had%200.04%20deaths%20per%20100%2C000.

control. Canada has five times fewer gun deaths per person than the US, and Canada is considered quite violent by European standards, since Canada has twice as many as Europe's average.

Are there countries where you have a higher chance of dying by gunshot than the US? Yes. Countries like Mexico, swamped by drug gangs, and Venezuela, overrun by a ruthless dictatorship, have even higher gun death rates than the US.

According to CDC statistics based on death certificates, in 2017 there were 39,773 people killed by guns in the US. The number has been growing since 2000. The numbers are highest in conservative states such as Alabama and Arkansas, lowest in liberal states with stricter laws, such as California and New York, despite the concentration of gangs and huge cities there[48].

Most of those are criminals shooting criminals. Should we bother to care, if this is true? I think we should. In my first five years living in the US, I met two people who had friends or family killed as innocent bystanders. I have met several people who told me of friends or family killed by gunshots from their domestic partners. Even if we didn't care about the criminals, there are too many innocents caught in the American crossfire.

Firearms are the leading cause of death for American children and teens. More than 1,700 children and teens die by gun homicide every year. For children under the age of 13, these gun homicides most frequently occur in the home and are often connected to domestic or family violence. Approximately three million American children witness gun violence every year.

Women in the U.S. are 21 times more likely to be killed with a gun than women in other high-income countries (see

[48] Homicide Mortality by State, CDC, March 2022.
https://www.cdc.gov/nchs/pressroom/sosmap/homicide_morta
lity/homicide.htm

article in *Preventive Medicine*, 2019, issue 123). In an average month, 53 American women are shot to death by an intimate partner.

Most gun deaths are suicides. True. According to death certificates, about 60% of gun deaths are suicides. I had drinks in December 2019 with a doctor from Texas, who spent a lot of time in emergency wards. As a department director at a medical school, he studied causes of death. He told me that most suicide attempts are "gestures", like the woman who takes an overdose of pills and then immediately calls 911, or the man who cuts his wrists just before a friend is expected to visit. The problem with guns is that the gesture is usually fatal. 51% of suicides in the US use a gun, since guns are so easy to come by here. If there were 20% fewer guns in the US, there should be close to 20% fewer successful suicides.

Don't worry: as white middle class, your chances of getting shot are very low, since it's mostly black people getting shot. Should this matter? Setting that aside, it is true: the chances of getting shot if you are black are 14-30 times higher than if you are white, depending on education level (according to The Lancet, June 1, 2019). Even so, the chance of a white person being shot and killed in the US is approximately twice as high as it is in Canada, where it is twice as high as in Europe.

"Active shooter incidents" have been rising steadily since 2000. These are defined by the FBI as "one or more individuals actively engaged in killing or attempting to kill people in a populated area." That affects everyone, not just our African American friends. My reasons to wish for more control of guns in the US are not just about increasing my own chances of survival. Our laws should not be here just to protect white middle class Americans. If 100% of gun deaths in this country were blacks, it should still be just as high a priority to reduce that 39 thousand.

The Constitution says we have the right to own guns. The Democrats are trying to take away our rights to even own hunting rifles. I hear this only from Republicans, not from any Democrat I've ever discussed this with. Taking away hunting rifles is not on any Democrat's agenda that I know of. Maybe there is a tiny minority of Democrats who actually want to overturn the Second Amendment, but this is not the position of the two thirds of Americans who want reasonable gun control. Hunters, feel free to keep all your rifles. According to the FBI, 64% of gun murders in the US involve hand guns. Hunting rifles are the very least of America's gun problems; hunters tend to be careful with their firearms, and the only people typically hurt by them are themselves, their children, or their hunting partners, and all of those are relatively rare.

If everybody had a gun, criminals would not be able to murder so easily. The solution to the number of gun deaths in America is more guns.

Fox News covered covered the Dec 29, 2019 church shooting in White Settlement, near Dallas, of a man who shot two people dead before being shot himself, not as three tragic gun deaths, but as a triumph of concealed carry. The first shooter had a long history of violence and mental problems.

Statistically it is obvious, looking around the world, that more guns means more gun deaths, not the other way around. But for a moment, let's skip the statistics of American children getting killed more often than in any rich country, and look at that one incident in Texas. I see two ways to look at it. First, thanks to lots of people in the church having guns, the shooter was brought down quickly. A hero with a gun shot him. Without all those guns, the shooter might have killed a lot more people before some brave hero tackled him, or he shot himself, or just stopped shooting.

Another way to look at it is to imagine the shooter did not have a gun, in the same way that a repeatedly drunk driver with a record of consistently driving on the wrong side of the road would not have a car. The two innocents who died would be alive today.

I think both ways of looking at the White Settlement shooting are accurate. But in one of them, three people died including two innocents, and in the other, nobody dies.

The guns used in murders are mostly illegal, so gun control legislation won't decrease the murder rate.

The first part of this is true, according to the Department of Justice (Special Report NCJ251776, January 2019), which found 56% of firearm offenses involved stolen, found, or black market guns. This does not mean gun control has no effect on murder rate. 56% illegal means 44% were "legal guns." Countries and states and cities which put universal background checks in place see reductions of 15% in the number of murders, according to studies by the FBI and CDC (see Boston University's The Brink, Aug 6, 2019). That's the direct effect of putting the background checks in place. If you look overall at states with and without background checks, the difference in firearm homicide rates is even higher, at 58%.

Keep your guns, and buy as many as you like, if you are willing to prove you're a competent, safe gun owner, and use your guns responsibly. The Second Amendment should stand, as a fundamental liberty for people to do as they choose, but as Scalia said, there are reasonable limits to every liberty.

6: GOVERNMENT DEBT AND TAXES

Many Americans think their taxes are too high. Let's start by examining how the US compares with other countries. Going from Wikipedia, checked by comparing with lists from several other sources:

- In first place, with a gut-churning 64% of GDP consumed by taxes, is Algeria. Nobody wants to be Algeria. Close behind are Timor-Leste and Afghanistan. Nobody wants to be them either.

- In places 4, 5, 6, and 7 are Norway, Finland, Denmark, and Sweden, with 50-54% of GDP consumed by taxes. Denmark is often measured as the happiest country on Earth. Norway by some measures is the richest. All of them have health care for 100% of their population. They also have some extremely rich people, like the family behind

IKEA, or the creators of Skype. Because of these, I don't think anyone can claim high taxes are definitively bad for a country.

- In 9th place is France. Their taxes take up 48% of GDP, and there is much to complain about. Their taxes on the rich are awfully high. Perhaps this is too much. But the average French person is healthier than the average American, thanks to the top-ranked health care system in the world, less stress, and perhaps more red wine. There are about 38 billionaires in France, similar to Switzerland, South Korea, and Australia, so the high taxes have not obliterated the ability to get very rich.

- In 24th place is Portugal. 37% of their money goes to taxes. I went there on vacation last year; it is a wonderful place; people across the country seemed genuinely happy and free. Portugal is proud of its culture and democracy and human rights.

- In 36th place is the United Kingdom, at 34%. Brits love to complain about their weather, about losing all the time in World Cup soccer, about being part of Europe, about leaving Europe, and many other things. Perhaps they complain about taxes, but in several years of working in London and outlying cities in the UK, I did not hear it. Perhaps they get their money's worth for that 34%.

- We are still a long way from getting down to the incredibly low taxes of the United States. Stay tuned.

- In 46th place, at a mere 32% of GDP, is the country of my birth: Canada. Canada is very proud of its system of government. US News and World Report ranked Canada the second best country in the world, based on a poll of 20,000 random people. (The US was not #1.) The median

Canadian is about as well off as the median American, depending on the year you look, even though America has far more wealth overall — the money is distributed more equally north of the border. This doesn't prevent Canadians from getting extremely rich; at last count there are 41 billionaires there, and at least 200,000 millionaires, growing by about 20,000 millionaires per year, as of 2019.

- In 50th place is Albania, a very poor country in Europe. We are getting down to the very-low tax countries, where total taxes in the country consume less than 30% of the economy.

- In 57th place is Australia, at 28%.

- In 60th place is Romania, at just below 28%.

- At last, we arrive at 63rd place, with 27% of GDP consumed by taxes: the United States of America. The countries with even lower taxes overall include Kazakhstan, Mexico, Jordan, China, Venezuela, Singapore, Hong Kong, and in 180th and last place, the UAE.

Even though the US has among the lowest taxes in the world, and whether you consider them high or low, Americans do have the democratic right to decide how much of their GDP should be spent by government, and how much by companies or individuals. If Americans wants low government services with low taxes, that is their right. How should we decide the right amount? Here are some principles I would apply, at least to the US federal government budget:

- The budget deficit should average less than the growth in GDP, so if the economy is growing by 2% per year, the government debt should grow by no more than 2%. We can allow higher during recessions, as long as we budget lower during boom times. Sadly this principle hasn't been applied since Clinton's administration, when the budget was balanced (0% deficit). Bush and Trump tax cuts have led to the deficit being higher than economic growth every year since. After recovering from the 2008 financial crisis, Obama's administration got it down to 3.1% for 2016, his last year, pretty close to the growth rate, but it since bounced higher again with Trump's tax cuts, rising each year, to 4.6% in 2019, and over 7% with Biden's spending programss. It must be brought down to 3%, to avoid the sin of dumping debt as an inheritance for our children.

- Collection for social security and other government programs must be sustainable for the long term. Today's social security collection is well known to be insufficient to cover future retirees. Canada had the same problem in the 1990s and fixed it. The US Congress has hardly even debated the problem, let alone passed any related legislation.

- As a rich country, the US should be able to afford government services at least at the average level of the OECD, or perhaps a little lower. This definition is a bit vague, but Washington could make reasonable assessments. Just as many companies have their Human Resource departments determine what salaries to pay to be "at 50-75% of the market" or similar metrics, the US government could set goals to have Americans as well served as the average European.

- The US has a unique role as the only democratic superpower. This makes a strong US military, strong enough to defend against any aggression by China against US assets or allies, anywhere in the world, a vital priority. We have to pay for that.

If you agree with these principles, you must accept higher taxes. Not as high as France, but a little higher than they are today. Otherwise, do you accept a shrinking military that China can beat? Or continued malnutrition of poor American children? Or wiping out Social Security when it goes bankrupt in a few decades? Or passing a bankrupt government to our grandchildren?

Let's establish a careful, gradual, calibrated simplification of our taxes, and reasonable increase for those who can afford it (there are many in this rich country), so we can pay our bills. Since the US government is currently running significant deficits, and forecast to increase its deficits to bankruptcy levels without policy change, some combination of higher tax or lower spending is necessary.

Cutting taxes with the theory that growth would decrease the deficit has been tried three times in the last 30 years, by Reagan, Bush, and Trump, and failed each time. Their administrations saw larger increases in the deficit than the intervening Democrat-led administrations.

Perhaps you believe in cutting government spending. I do, if done well, but look at the largest chunks of spending in the federal government's budget, and I argue throughout this book that most of these should stay at the current level, not be cut:

1. Social Security, Unemployment, and Labor. Under the current rules, Social Security spending will grow, not shrink, massively, over the next few decades. See my proposals for improving this with a revenue-neutral approach (no higher taxes, no higher spending).
2. Medicare and Health. See my proposals in this book for getting government out of health care, for better quality, at the same or lower cost thanks to a free market.
3. Military, including Veterans' Benefits. I don't believe we should cut either of these.

The three categories above represent about 86% of federal

government spending. Everything else the government does is covered by just 14%, from education to research to embassies and consulates that support Americans overseas. They have all been increasingly squeezed as Social Security grew and tax rates shrank.

To get the government deficit under control, the US should increase some tax. What's the best way to increase taxation, for the least negative impact on the economy? Socialists like to push for wealth taxes or higher income tax rates for the rich, but these will not bring in much. Until the US cooperates with other countries to harmonize tax regimes worldwide, rich people will shift their income, or the profits of their companies, to other countries with lower taxes, and the IRS will not gain by increased rates.

My preference, and that of most economists worldwide, is to create a very small federal sales tax. The US is almost unique in having no federal sales tax. Some countries have as high as 20%. I would suggest 1%, so low it will not create a black market of people avoiding the tax, but with 70% of American GDP spent on consumption, an excellent way to balance the books.

Even better, if you hate any new tax, but believe the US should reduce its deficit, let's properly fund the IRS auditing branch. Charles Rettig, IRS commissioner, estimates the government loses about $1trn in tax revenues annually because of cheating (The Economist, Taxation in America, Apr 15, 2022). Never mind a tax increase, just fund the IRS appropriately, upgrade its 1960s computer system, and reap the windfalls.

7: REGULATION OVERLOAD

One concern of American conservatives is government over-regulation. Businesses can make more money, and people are more free to pursue happiness, if there are fewer regulations in the way.

There are indeed a lot of regulations in America. According to the Office of the Federal Register, by 1998 there were 134,723 pages of federal regulations in effect. Congress passes about 200 laws per year, and then federal agencies create 20-30 rules for each law, to implement the details, leading to thousands more pages added every year.

There have been many efforts to reduce the load. President Clinton issued Executive Order 12866 in 1993, which governs what federal agencies must do before rules take effect. For all regulations, a detailed cost-benefit analysis must be performed. Regulations with an estimated cost of $100 million or more are designated "major rules," and require completion of a more detailed Regulatory Impact Analysis (RIA). The RIA must justify the cost of the new regulation and must be approved by the Office of Management and Budget (OMB) before the regulation can take effect. Despite this, since 1993 there have been between 42 and 105 new "major rules" each year. There has been no significant difference between Democrat and Republican administrations, with the exception of Trump: under him, the number of new laws and regulations dropped roughly in half, while the number of pages of new regulations dropped by 25%.

There is broad bipartisan support for the idea of requiring two rules to be dropped for every new rule added. Within days of his inauguration, President Trump issued an Executive Order requiring it. I like the idea, and would take it further, arguing that at least two pages of regulation be retired, for every one page added. This will prevent bureaucrats from adding a rule that runs on for 50 pages while cutting one page with several "smaller" rules. I believe it should still be relatively easy to find obsolete or poor regulations to discard, among those 134,723 pages.

But let's not throw the baby out with the bath water. Many, perhaps even most of those federal regulations are good for America. They include, for example, requiring food packaging to list ingredients, cars to have air bags, baby seats to be safety-tested, and dangerous chemicals not to be used in workplaces. Some day we will run out of bad regulations to dispose of. That is a political decision. Yes, while Republicans run the administration, a Republican viewpoint will drive many decisions about regulations to add or delete, and similarly during Democratic administrations. Fortunately, Americans have a free press that lets them know what the administration is doing, and a chance every four years to decide if they're going too far.

There is an argument to put an expiry date on any new regulation, to make sure they don't stay on the books long after their utility or morality no longer make sense. I'm not in favor of this, because too many things can go wrong as a result. Partisan logjams could cause a vital regulation to lapse. The uncertainty of a regulation's renewal could have huge impacts on industrial investments. Requiring retirement of old regulations, with cost-benefit analysis of new ones, should be enough of a force to continually improve the base.

8: FAKE NEWS

I fondly remember when I was a child, our family watching Walter Cronkite of CBS News every weekday evening, to see and hear what was going on in the world. There was trust that the broadcast news, as well as newspapers, told the truth, and that journalists would seek out the stories that people wanted to know about. Some people didn't bother with the news, but generally, if you wanted to know about the political issues of the day, you could get the facts from the three big TV networks, or a newspaper, or a variety of radio stations.

Is that true today? If it isn't, what should we do about it? Part of me shudders at the thought of trying to "fix" journalism with political action. The worst countries on Earth share a characteristic: government control of media. Look at the descent of many thriving nations into miseries of poverty and persecution, and the earliest signs are government impeding the free press, first by a little, and then by a lot. In Venezuela, for example. Hugo Chavez first won power in 1998 with 56% of the vote in an election overseen by international observers, and widely recognized as fair. In that year, 88% of Venezuelan TV channels were independent. Chavez was popular, and Venezuela's economy was growing rapidly. Indeed it grew even faster until 2010, as an enlightened democracy. But Chavez did not want to lose power, so he steadily tightened the screws on Venezuela's press. Today, there is no Venezuelan media critical of Chavez' successor Nicolas Maduro, and the people are literally starving. Several countries are following Venezuela's example, such as Hungary, Austria, and Turkey. Of course the established dictatorships all long ago subdued their journalists, and continue to persecute any independent voices.

The First Amendment to the US Constitution guarantees the Freedom of the Press. So is there a problem in America? Why fix what isn't broken?

Ironically in the year I started this book, I heard almost identical complaints from my Trump-supporting friends as I did from Bernie Sanders' supporters: "You just can't trust anything you read these days." This is a common response when I mention facts to these friends, and by facts I mean statements about the world which have been verified by evidence, with multiple independent people working to prove or disprove them. In America in particular there is widespread feeling that nobody can be believed, that the objective truth is elusive, and in particular that the left or right wing media, whichever is on the opposite side from you, is full of lies and misdirection.

Fake news and conspiracy theories spread through social media have indeed risen to become a major cause of death[49]. Covid deaths in the US could have fallen to a trickle by June 2021 were it not for anti-vaccine lies. Over 30,000 Americans needlessly died of Covid in August 2021, at least 99% of which could have been spared by the effective vaccines widely available by then.

---

49 It's not hyperbole to say misinformation kills. For example, read "It's all connected, man" in The Economist of Sep 4, 2021, which reviews how conspiracy theories fueled massacres in The Congo, and hundreds of thousands of Covid-19 deaths that vaccination could have prevented.

Today, there is no lack of good journalism, and the US has a vociferous free press, but I worry that a shrinking minority of Americans seek unbiased journalism, and that a growing majority of Americans obtain information from heavily biased media, including sources such as Facebook posts that do not meet the definition of "journalism" and are indeed fake news, created by anonymous foreign and domestic agents with a political purpose. As a result, newspapers and radio stations and video journalists increasingly work for organizations with a strong political slant. Republicans go to Fox for their news, and Democrats go to CNN or the New York Times. Catering to their polarized audiences rather than prioritizing journalistic impartiality, media organizations have become increasingly editorial, mixing opinion pieces amongst news articles until they are difficult to distinguish from each other. Even within the "news" articles, bias is obvious. One of the following is a June 2020 headline from Fox News, the other a June 2020 headline from CNN. I presume the majority of Americans can guess which is which:

- "Ex-NYPD commish Bernie Kerik on Atlanta shooting: Tell 'thugs' to not 'attack our police'"
- "History says Trump's low approval rating is unlikely to move"

I wager the majority of readers could tell Fox from CNN by the photos they publish of Trump, without needing to read a word of the article.

Rupert Murdoch created Fox News in 1996 specifically in order to provide a conservative point of view, as he saw the American media at the time as having too much liberal bias. Fox does not thrive by having a dictatorial government choke off other media, but because it is the most popular with cable viewers. When I want to understand what American conservatives are thinking about an issue, I don't go to the New York Times or CNN, I go to Fox News or the Wall Street Journal.

I believe there continues to be a market for unbiased news in the US, although it's smaller than it used to be. Whether right or wrong, the American free market can decide. Any American who seeks out truth on political issues of the day can still find it, reading a plethora of opinions and facts, from a host of competing media, fact-checking each other. No politician in the US can act egregiously without media on one side or the other publishing the facts. No sordid truth can long be hidden, for any American who cares to read both sides. If many Americans on left and right choose to read only one side, that is their loss but their right.

I am left with one worry, not about journalists, but about other players in the information market. When a politician or other social media influencer publicly makes a false statement, we can count on journalists to fact-check it, and counter it with the other side of the story. Every politician lies at least occasionally, as fact-checkers have proven repeatedly. Every time Hilary Clinton lied, Americans could count on Fox News to prove it, and to vigorously make it known. Similarly, CNN published daily updates on the lies in Trump's twitter account. There are websites which rank politicians on the percentage of their public statements that are lies; you can compare Trump versus Biden truthfulness analytically and factually every day, if you want. This is all as it should be. If you don't want to hear negative news about the Democrats, don't watch Fox. If you don't want to hear negative news about Trump, don't watch CNN. If you want the whole truth, watch both.

But what about less public lies? Russian interference in US elections, for example, often consists of targeted Facebook posts or ads, aimed at particular types of voter. Mailing lists from left and right wing groups send heavily biased statements to targeted voters, sometimes full of falsehoods, hoping to maintain or sway their votes. Some of these include cunningly disguised lies. I believe in freedom of speech, including even the freedom to lie, but let's make sure our journalists at least have a chance to refute them. I would hope a law could be passed, which required that every political statement sent to large numbers of people, say over 100, must be made available to the full public, giving journalists and other citizens a chance to fact-check it, and tag it with counter-arguments. Right and left wing groups could continue to feel free to send targeted ads... but opposing groups should get a chance to argue.

Some social media platforms might argue this is too hard to manage, but there is an existence proof: Wikipedia. Even the most politically sensitive topics addressed by Wikipedia generally result in balanced, fact-based, reliably accurate articles. How? Wikipedia spends less on content-review than FaceBook, by a huge margin, but has a well-defined process for publishers to resolve conflicts and reach consensus. Articles that are still contentious are flagged as such.

Why not require all social media to implement some form of the Wikipedia policies? This would not eliminate fake news entirely, but in practice would mean that most fake news would at least come with a warning label.

9: EDUCATION

While America has 8 of the world's 10 best universities, its kindergarten through high school (K-12) education consistently scores well below the leading countries. For example, 40% of high schools in NYC do not teach chemistry, physics or upper-level algebra[50]

As a result, America is less and less the land of opportunity, and more and more the land of inherited privilege. The children of the rich half of America get far better educations than the children of the poor half, and so the rich get richer, and the poor don't. I like a free market, and say the rich should get to spend their money on education if they want, but the minimum standard of education in the US is far too low for the health of our economy and culture.

This is fundamentally because education is about 50% paid for by local property taxes, so is dramatically uneven across the nation. Overall, despite federal and state subsidies to attempt

---

[50] The Economist, January 11, 2020

rebalancing, the poorest schools get less than half the money per child as the richest[51]. In successful countries, the main source of K-12 funding is state-level.

Yes the number one factor for a child's success in K-12 is positive parental involvement, but classroom size, quality of teachers, availability of classes, and basic facilities matter too. These need money.

I would propose a new federal program of transfers to the states, specifically for states to spend on improving their poorer schools. The money would come with conditions, that it must be spent directly on the poorer schools, raising them to a published minimum spending level per student, consistent with a world class education. The exact methods would be left to the states, per current state responsibility for education. This program could be paid for by the removal of oil industry subsidies, the slowly growing carbon tax, and a very small federal sales tax, as I discuss in other chapters. In the long run, a better educated American population will be more productive and healthy, but that will take years to realize. The minimum standard for K-12 spending may start low while the carbon tax is low, but I would favor some ambition here.

A chapter on education in the US would be incomplete if it ignored charter schools, private schools, religion, and sex education. While I believe the key education issue in America is the underfunding of poor schools, I have an opinion on each of these as well.

First, in the spirit of a free market, I support the existence of charter and private schools, as long as they meet rigorously monitored standards that will make the worst school in the US at least "good enough" by international standards. To improve education, there should be experiments in different ways to teach, and organize teaching. To support individual freedom or religion and other choices, parents should not be prevented

51

https://www.usatoday.com/story/money/business/2015/10/03/24-7-wall-st-richest-poorest-school-districts/73205874/

from supporting religious schools, or other options, including diversion of their children's share of government spending on education.

Yes there is a "but". Such schools may teach Christianity or Islam or Judaism or any other religion, as long as they also teach all the fundamentals of Humanities and Science. They can teach Creationism as long as they teach the science of evolution. They can teach abstinence as long as they also provide comprehensive sex education. Let all our children learn as much as possible, and make their own value decisions, guided by their upbringing but also a wide set of teachings to choose from.

I talk about sex education in another chapter, but please accept a bit of repetition here in the context of K-12 education. I think all Americans agree we should try to reduce the number of abortions as much as possible. Overwhelming evidence shows the best way to reduce abortions is to provide thorough sex education before and during puberty, with convenient access to birth control for all ages. Some states have tried teaching abstinence, with the result of far higher rates of teenage pregnancy and abortions than sister states. Alas, I may lose conservative readers here who feel it's a higher priority to prevent teenage sex, and simply try to prevent abortions by outlawing them... but the results are extremely clear – that approach leads to more pregnancies and more abortions. I think any conservative who chooses to research the facts will choose better sex education and contraception, as an add-on to promoting abstinence.

10: STUDENT LOANS AND TUITION

Bernie Sanders is beloved by many, and hated by others, for his radical socialist platform, far beyond what the Democratic Party espouses. One of his favorite planks is to make public universities in America tuition free, and forgive all student debt. This idea has generated storms of debate, with some loving it for the relief of debt, and others hating it for the $2.2 trillion tax increase. Bernie published a plan for paying for it, and the $2.2 trillion is his estimate, with about $1.6 trillion being the current student loan debt. The tax would be on Wall Street transactions, which would of course lead to smart money shifting those transactions elsewhere, and with that large a bill, significantly hurting the American economy.

I know young people who are scraping by, crushed and depressed by student loans. That doesn't help grow the economy. It makes sense to address the problem, along with the equality of opportunity to get a college degree, and to kill three birds with one stone, to make sure Americans are appropriately educated for great jobs in the future. Let's find a way to do it without trillions of dollars in extra taxes.

My favorite approach is to have people pay for their higher education, to the extent their family income allows, and that includes paying off student loans. Tuition and loan repayment could both be a percentage of income. Colleges could compete with higher or lower percentages. Let's say a particular state university charges 3%. A family sending their daughter there, the year after her parents made $200,000, would pay $6,000. A boy with zero-income parents and nothing to his name but good enough grades would pay $0. A million-a-year rock star will pay $30,000 to go back to the same school.

Post secondary education is expensive in the US[52]. The university system is the best in the world, and it works hard to provide scholarships and loans to enable bright students of all races and classes worldwide to benefit, but student loan debt in the US remains crippling. Universities are the lifeblood of research and education beyond the basics of K-12, and are as essential to the power of the nation as they are to the benefit of the students paying for their education[53]. This is to say the country needs university-educated people, that there is a reason to invest in universities, for a government.

Even if your tuition is zero or cheap, you have to buy rent and food while getting through college. Maybe you can work enough to cover them, or maybe you'll get student loans. I suggest student loan repayments be set about 10% of income, until they're paid off. That means a successful medical doctor who graduates with $400,000 of debt will pay it off pretty quickly, while a struggling artist with a Fine Arts degree who

---

52 Forbes magazine – American college spending vs. other

countries:https://www.forbes.com/sites/prestoncooper2/2019/09/22/america-spends-more-on-college-than-virtually-any-other-country/?sh=40d3492a3348

53 Comprehensive statistical analysis and literature review on the economic impacts of universities. https://www.sciencedirect.com/science/article/pii/S0272775718300414

doesn't make it in Hollywood might pay $2000 per year for the rest of their life, but nobody suffers terribly for the debt, and everyone pays for the amount of higher education they personally choose to pursue.

Here are some of the advantages of the percentage approach to both tuition and student loan repayment:

- We don't have to increase taxes one penny, to make this happen.
- Students will be motivated to get a worthwhile education, because they have to pay for it. A more expensive degree might be worth the investment of their time and money, or it may not, and they'll have to figure out that trade off.
- Our brilliant and talented poorest students will be able to go to college, and become far more productive citizens as a result.
- Everyone with the drive to attend college can do so, even if they and their parents are dirt poor.

There is another view I'd like to give my opinion on. Some say a college education is becoming essential for everyone in society, to get any decent kind of job, or to enjoy life with any sense of fulfillment, and therefore government should pay for it entirely, as it does for primary and secondary education. Hundreds of years ago, no schooling was required to work the farm. Today, the simplest jobs any American citizen will generally contemplate require a high school education, and so we pay for high schools for all Americans. Should we go that far with higher education?

I think we may get there eventually, but are not there now. Today almost exactly 2/3 of American high school graduates head for college. Although some of the one third who don't would love to if it weren't for the cost, a lot of them don't want college, and are perfectly capable of making enough money other ways. Spending more years and money after high school is very much a choice, and I prefer not to force the choice of paying for it on everyone who pays taxes. There are inexpensive higher education choices, such as six month diplomas, that are great investments for some people who get a career out of it, and there are very expensive ones, like a PhD in Medicine, which require a dedication I'd like to see proven by having skin in the game, rather than have my tax dollars pay for anyone to give it a go at zero cost to them. The range of choices in higher education, unlike high school, to me make it better served by a system where the beneficiary pays for it.

Universities serve society in many other ways, in addition to turning high school graduates into professionals. University research is the deep root of innovation and progress in a country, with spin-off companies driving growth. It's not a coincidence that the US has the most Nobel Prizes of any country, as well as the most successful high tech companies. It's not a coincidence that the US funds more university research than any other country, and has the most dynamic industrial economy as well. University research leads to more ideas, more innovation, more new products, more new ways of doing things, that make a country better. So in addition to making sure our brightest young minds can get the education they want, we need to keep our university system the best in the world, to drive the new ideas a country needs to thrive. This doesn't require a change, just a continuation: the US federal government has spent about 0.4% of GDP on research, pretty steadily since before 1970.

Furthermore, beyond training our professionals, and doing research, universities stimulate freedom of thought, and the continual intellectual revolutions that make for human progress. We don't want Americans to be docile factory workers, unthinking patriots who parrot the government way. We want rebelliousness, fomenting new ideas constantly, and people who think the government is wrong and should be changed for the better. Perhaps you are a conservative who doesn't like the sound of that. Perhaps you think universities today are far too liberal, and train our youth to forget good values. In addition, you are supported by lots of evidence that universities have become so "politically correct" that conservative voices are unwelcome on campus, and freedom of speech is threatened. I think the answer to that is not reduced funding for universities, which would be shooting ourselves in the foot. The answer is more freedom of speech. Court cases can force universities to allow Christian groups to speak and act however they wish on campus, to invite conservative speakers as often as liberal ones, and not to ban anyone from speaking. Conservatives should battle for their voices to be heard, through persuasive argument, and win the bright minds of liberal youth. "Cancel culture" must be fought in the courts, not by a competing "censorship culture" that prevents liberal speech.

Another role for universities, beyond training and research and freedom of thought, is providing society with passionate vocations. I believe this will grow increasingly important in coming decades, as automation replaces more and more menial jobs. GDP will continue to rise, standards of living will rise, but people will need something meaningful to do with their time, rather than count on a job to fill most of their daylight. Universities are a natural place for that, full of ideas and learning and activities. They should not be for the rich elite; they should be for everyone. Everyone should have the chance to learn something new, find something new to get passionate about, and become better at it. Yes there are other avenues besides university, but post-secondary education already today covers fine arts, music, literature, dance, theater, science, engineering, languages, psychology, philosophy, social sciences, history, and a thousand other pursuits. Let's keep those roads open for everyone to explore.

Speaking of keeping the roads open, in this country, we have to talk about admissions and race. Again, as on so many other issues, the US is nearly alone with this thorny problem. Should admissions favor disadvantaged groups, to make up for past sins and create a more balanced society? I don't think this is an easy decision. If you force admissions to go purely on test scores, universities will be very heavily weighted to Asian minorities, and black youth who suffered terrible schools their entire lives will have very little chance. Perhaps it's meritocratic and right that the entire graduating class of the entire Ivy League include no white or black people, if the Asians can earn every spot, but I don't think it makes for an ideal America. If you tilt the playing field with subjective or other criteria, you risk making the selection racist, and disadvantaging students who worked hard to earn their place.

I honestly don't know what the right policy would be. Perhaps this doesn't matter, because whatever laws or regulations or policies are propounded, the Supreme Court is going to weigh in and decide legitimacy based on overriding laws and precedent. But to the extent I could influence it, I'd advocate at least some affirmative action, to partially level the playing field particularly for disadvantaged black Americans, until the K-12 school system is fixed to not heavily weigh against them. I hope we can fix K-12 within a few years. We could. We should.

11: IMMIGRATION

What is the right number of immigrants, and how should the US decide which ones to allow? Even under the Trump administration, the United States ranked #1 in the world for immigrants, with just over one million legal immigrants per year. Per capita, the US ranks lower. Here are some net migration numbers per 100,000 population for large and medium size countries, according to the CIA, as of 2017, including legal and illegal, immigration balanced against emigration:

1)	Spain	7.8
2)	Norway	5.9
3)	Canada	5.7
4)	Australia	5.5
5)	Belgium	5.4
6)	Sweden	5.3
7)	Austria	4.8
8)	Switzerland	4.7

9) Ireland   4.0
10) Iceland   4.0
11) United States 3.9 (per 100,000, in 2017)

Each country should choose its desired level of immigration, balancing their economy's appetite for workers, the fertility rate of citizens, preservation of values, and of course, a measure of human kindness toward refugees. What is the right number for the US? Opinions are all over the map, in both parties.

As I write this paragraph, I'm on vacation in Costa Rica, one of the happiest countries on Earth, and a terrific tourist destination. Costa Rica is relatively well off, with a minimum wage of $700 per month, but an average standard of living much higher than you'd think from that number. In a country of 5 million people, almost 1 million Nicaraguans obtain work visas and live here for 6 months, renewing repeatedly. They tend to earn the Costa Rica minimum wage, and do jobs the locals won't, or don't need to anymore. One tour guide told me they have all the same issues as America does, with Nicaraguans working illegally for even less, mostly in construction, but it seems to largely be win-win for Costa Rican's as well as the much poorer Nicaraguans.

Canada absorbs twice as many immigrants per person as the US and has for decades. In fact, Canada has approximately quadrupled its immigration over the past few years, and now has nearly as many immigrants as the US, despite having one tenth the population! Canadian culture has grown stronger and more unified over that time. I don't believe the US is straining at some excessive level of immigration, and a majority of Americans agree[54]. As of 2021, only 33% of Americans polled said they want less immigration.

There are many types of immigrants. Let's talk separately

---

54 Today 29% of Americans want more, 38% want to maintain current levels, and 33% want less -- Cato Institute, Apr 27, 2021. https://www.cato.org/survey-reports/e-pluribus-unum-findings-cato-institute-2021-immigration-identity-national-survey

about refugees, workers, family members, investors, and unauthorized residents, starting with that last one.

Unauthorized Residents

First a few words about words. As a foreigner I was ignorant of how loaded immigration terminology is in the US. Now I've learned that saying "illegal alien" firmly identifies you as an extreme Republican who probably wants all of them deported, while saying "undocumented immigrant" firmly identifies you as an extreme Democrat who probably wants open borders. Sigh. My apologies if you use these terms and have more moderate views. I searched for a "neutral" term that is reasonably acccurate, and thanks to an early reader of Hope, I've come to use "unauthorized resident".

The number of people crossing the southern border illegally was dropping for decades. Because of this, the Trump administration never deported or arrested as many people in any year as the Obama administration, not for lack of trying, but because the number of illegal attempts continued to drop. Net migration between the US and Mexico was negative from 2007 until Covid — more leaving than coming. A 2015 study performed by demographers of the University of Texas at San Antonio and the University of New Hampshire found that immigration from Mexico, both legal and illegal, peaked in 2003 and that from the period between 2003 and 2007 to the period of 2008 to 2012, immigration from Mexico decreased 57%. The net total number of unauthorized residents in the US peaked at about 12 million in 2007 and fell steadily for years, to about 10 million as of 2018. Over 80% of those 10 million have lived in the US for over 10 years.

But then came Covid, and the worsening of life in Central America, especially in Venezuela. From 2021 to the Spring of 2024 we saw a surge of people try to cross Mexico and enter the US, coming from a wide and growing range of countries.

When the last dictatorship on our planet is finally swept away by the will of its people, and every nation on Earth enjoys a government chosen by its people, migration across our southern border will no longer be a problem. But until then, that border is too attractive.

With the American economy in its second decade of expansion, only briefly interrupted by the pandemic, and unemployment at record lows (except for a temporary surge during Covid), the US can use all the immigrants currently arriving at its borders, but I am not suggesting the US throw open its borders, unlike some of the more extreme Democrats. Illegal entry should be deterred, with money spent to get it back down to a trickle. How? Here's what one friend suggested.

Coordinate a massive military style assault on the drug cartels and criminal gangs across Central America, in cooperation with federal governments to the south that will support our efforts. Do not give money to these governments directly (past experience says this would be foolish), but provide intelligence, and send our troops and military capabilities where necessary to fight the war on drugs that are causing local citizens to flee, and the product of which is killing thousands of Americans each year.

Two, instead of a border wall, build extensive facilities along the border to provide decent but basic housing for the migrants crossing the border, for up to a year. Give them temporary jobs even if it is to assist local, state or the Federal governments. For example, they can help build more border facilities in exchange for housing, health care, meals, and education. No free handouts. They can participate in growing food locally for the facilities. Children will be required to attend school. Everyone who can contribute to society will be required to make a contribution. Require mandatory preparation and education for eventually leaving the new facilities so they will be best prepared to become productive residents elsewhere in the US. In addition to being vetted, there will be guidelines and standards to determine when the person is prepared to freely move about the interior of the US and fend for themselves. This would be available to all who legally present themselves at the border for thorough vetting.

For those that tried to cross illegally, I would institute a policy of immediate deportation. If you want to come to the US, don't start off by breaking US laws.

This leaves open the huge question of what to do about unauthorized residents already in the US. According to Pew Research as well as the Department of Homeland Security, that number peaked around 2007, when it was at 12.2 million and 4% of the total U.S. population. Estimates in 2016 put the number of unauthorized immigrants at 10.7 million, representing 3.3% of the total U.S. population. The conservative opinion has been to find and deport them. Obama's government deported more aliens than any previous or subsequent administration, although it prioritized criminals and recent arrivals. What would be best for the United States? More deportations, including Dreamers? Or less? Even if they could all be identified and found, would the US be better or worse off deporting them? For those sponging welfare money, stealing, killing, or otherwise hurting America, of course they should be jailed and deported. That tiny minority who do such things should be searched for and deported. The rest are working, contributing to the American economy, supporting themselves and others. They should all be given work visas, and like a green card holder, a chance to apply for citizenship after five years of good behavior. During that five years they can contribute to social security and taxes, but not be eligible for any government benefits.

Would this encourage more illegal entry? To discourage that, it could be a one-time visa grant, written into law for at least twenty years, along with tougher penalties for illegal entry to the US. Yes I'm aware this is exactly the deal that was made decades ago, a deal that was broken as enforcement wasn't implemented. Aware of that history, let's write the new amnesty with teeth to prevent a relapse. The work visas would be revokable in case US unemployment rises above some threshold, and dependent on the person maintaining employment, getting a new job within a short period of time, should they lose their current one.

I call this a work visa, not an amnesty, but let's tackle the objections anyway, for those who might consider this visa equivalent to an amnesty. The ones I have heard are dislike for rewarding illegal behavior, Mexicans taking jobs from Americans, and draining of welfare or similar government resources. Let's consider each of these.

1. Rewarding unauthorized residency. As noted above, a one-time visa grant for the good of America's economy can avoid encouraging illegal residency by writing into law that no such visa will be granted again for 20 years. Also, to counter the "reward" let their be a hefty fine or fee for every unauthorized resident, as part of the visa, which they can pay off over their lifetime. Say $20,000.

2. Taking jobs. There is no lack of jobs in the US. To a certain point, the more workers we have, the more jobs get created, and the bigger our economy grows, supporting American preeminence in the world. Yes, if unemployment ever grows above 10% again, and Americans truly struggle to find work, worker visas could be revoked and immigrants sent away, but for now, they are a benefit not a negative.

3. Taking government resources. I was quite surprised to hear a young black woman in Milwaukee say she supports Trump. Not a large percentage of black Americans voted for him. But her position was based on her belief that immigrants get free government money, taking resources away that Americans can't access. If that were true, I would understand the anger. Fortunately, it's a lie. The Republican Congress laws of 1996 that Bill Clinton signed made almost all welfare payments ineligible for immigrants, and they remain that way. A comprehensive study of immigration in 2015 funded by Homeland Security and others found 86% of first generation immigrant males are in the labor force, higher than native-born Americans. They

also have fewer health problems, and even get divorced less. By the second generation, they contribute $30 billion more in taxes than they receive in benefits[55]. It is, however, true that school systems across the US do educate the children of unauthorized residents.

America was built by immigrants, and its free enterprise system thrives with ongoing immigration. On average, immigrants pay more taxes, create more companies, and obtain more patents than native-born Americans.

Refugees and Applicants for Asylum

As with most forms of immigration, the US has long been #1 in refugees. Until 2018, the US had always accepted the largest absolute number of refugees in the world, and usually more than all other countries combined. President Trump reduced the number of refugees accepted, so in 2018 Canada, with 1/10th the population of the US, took over as the country accepting the most refugees. Even with the cutbacks, though, the US was still #2.

How about per capita? The US is a large country, so of course it can handle more refugees than a small one. Per million people in the country, here are some numbers of accepted refugees, according to data from the Pew Research Center:

Canada	756
Australia	510
Sweden	493
Norway	465
United States	70

Is the US overwhelmed with foreign-born residents, legal or otherwise? Have a look at the following table of countries,

55www.nap.edu/catalog/21746/the-integration-of-immigrants-into-american-society, 2015 by National Academy of Sciences.

ranked by the percentage of foreign-born residents. This comes from Wikipedia, attributed to a United Nations report from 2015. I have left out lots of tiny countries that have very high immigrant populations, keeping just the top two of these. Note this includes unauthorized immigrants.

Country	Percentage Foreign-Born	Rank
Vatican City	100%	1
UAE	83.7%	2
Singapore	42.9%	22
Australia	33.3%	27
Saudi Arabia	31.1%	34
Switzerland	28.9%	37
Israel	26.5%	39
New Zealand	25.1%	42
Canada	21.9%	48
Kazakhstan	21.1%	49
Sweden	18.5%	53
Austria	17.4%	56
Germany	14.9%	66
United States	14.3%	67

Taking a look at the countries above the United States in this list, I do not see many disasters.

The UN estimates there are 26 million internationally displaced people worldwide, including Syrians escaping to Turkey, Rohingya fleeing genocide in Myanmar, and Venezuelans escaping the collapse of their country. Only a tiny fraction of these obtain legal invitations to remain in a new country. Even Canada's "open arms" take in less than 1/10th of 1% of the world's refugees each year.

Because the US is oceans away from Syria or Myanmar, the bulk of its refugees come across the Mexican border. But that number has been declining for decades. Why? One reason fewer and fewer Mexicans risk their lives to cross the border is that Mexico's standard of living has risen enough that staying home is a good option. If Honduras, El Salvador, Nicaragua, and Guatemala were as peaceful and productive as Costa Rica, the number of refugees crossing the Rio Grande would plummet.

Many people now arriving at the southern border attempting to immigrate to the US are women and children refugees from brutal regimes south of Mexico. The wall will not stop them; they seek out Customs and Border Protection staff to apply for refugee status. Of course the US need not accept all or any of them, but in the spirit of Ellis Island and the Statue of Liberty, I would be proud of America if it took in many of them, while at the same time working to make their home countries better places.

Despite all this, I do not advocate wide open borders. It makes sense to vet refugee applications as thoroughly as possible, to ferret out and deny entry to terrorists and other criminals, and not to give refugee status to people simply looking for a higher income. The US can lead the world in accepting refugees, but their should be a limit. Perhaps on a per capita basis the US could choose to be third, or tenth, or twentieth in the world, in the number of refugees it accepts. In 2017 it placed last in the Western World. Last place.

Legal Immigrant Workers

This category is close to my heart, as this is how I wound up in the US myself.

I've heard proposals to make immigration unlimited for educated professionals. I've heard variations such as allowing unlimited immigration among English-speaking countries for people with university degrees. I would not go that far.

I've heard President Trump's campaign promise to eliminate the H1B program, to stop the main source of professional immigrants. I think that would be going too far the other way.

What is the happy medium for America? How many new doctors, engineers, scientists, and other educated people should be allowed in? While I haven't pushed the Canadian model in most of this book's chapters, I do think the Canadian approach makes sense for America here: if the candidate has a legitimate job offer from an American company, let them in, as long as unemployment in that field is lower than some threshold, say 5%. Congress could review that threshold every two years.

Today, notwithstanding the pandemic crisis, American business has been held back by the H1B program's quota allowing as few as one quarter of professionals with job offers to come in, while unemployment for those professions is approximately 0%. Not quite every American computer programmer has a job, but well over 99% of them do, and American companies are pleading to bring more in, to grow American business even more. Congress has not adjusted the H1B quota since the program was created in 1990.

Family Member Immigrants

Once you have accepted someone as a new resident of America, whether as a refugee or a sports star, how much of their family should be allowed in as well? This is currently the largest category of immigrants, about 700,000 out of the million legal immigrants each year. Let's recap the rules here, with a view to adjusting them.

There are two kinds of family immigrant: "immediate relatives" which are unlimited, and "family preference" which have a quota and a long waiting list. Immediate relatives are the following, for a US citizen: spouse, unmarried child, adopted orphan child, or parent. I would change two things. First I would shift the parent category to the quota system of family preferences. Second I would allow the immediate relatives of permanent residents to come, not just citizens. Here's a story to illustrate how that would work. Under today's system, if Jimmy Chopra of India gets a US green card, he has to leave his wife behind for 5 years until he gets his US citizenship. That seems harsh. But once he has his citizenship, he can bring over his wife, and his parents. Then his wife can bring her parents, and the parents can bring all the younger siblings, and so on. Under the change I propose, Jimmy and his wife and children can all come with his green card, but his parents and siblings have to qualify themselves. I think this is fair, and of greater benefit to the US.

The second category, of "family preference", now includes adult children of citizens, spouses of green card holders, and siblings. The waiting lists are long. I think that's reasonable. We have to prioritize immigration somehow. Yes we can be kind to our citizens, and let them bring their extended family into the country, but the other types of immigrant, such as highly qualified professionals, and desperate refugees, should come first.

Some liberals as well as some conservatives may disagree with making it tougher to bring parents in. In many cultures, parents of adults are an indispensable part of the family, providing child care, home-making, family values, and wisdom. The family is weaker and less productive without them. I could be convinced, and leave parents in the "immediate relative" category. I'd like to hear more arguments on both sides.

Related to family immigration is the policy of birthright citizenship. As one anti-immigrant Democrat notes[56], most countries in the world do not grant citizenship automatically to a person born in their country, if the parents are not citizens. I don't think the US should either.

Investor Immigrants

This type of immigration works well, and in my humble opinion doesn't need any significant change. The "EB-5" visa is given to applicants who invest $1 million in the US, to create at least ten new jobs. This works out well for the US and brings

---

56 "How Many is Too Many" by Philip Cafaro, 2015, subtitled "The Progressive Argument for Reducing Immigration into the United States." I disagree with Cafaro's main thrust, but it's an interesting, provocative book, and I agree with his proposal to remove automatic birthright citizenship for children of non-citizens. I agree with him that the opinion of the majority of Americans that immigration should decrease must matter – but I'll argue to convince more Americans of the huge benefits of keeping immigration about where it is if not higher, and the painful dangers of shrinking it.

more successful people in to help our economy grow. It ain't broke, so let's not fix it.

The Right Number

So what's the right number for immigration to the US? Prior to the 2023/24 border surge, US immigration was about 1.2 million per year including about 200,000 unauthorized, quite low compared to other countries in per capita terms, but quite high compared to the past 100 years.

Here are some arguments for shrinking the number.

1. 81% of Americans want less immigration[57]. This is a powerful argument. We are, after all, a democracy. The poll also shows 79% of Americans want immigration to be more education and skill-based rather than family-based, and I would hope that changes to the type of immigration would change the support for higher numbers. If not, then we should be implementing the popular will.

2. Reduced immigration improves income equality, by creating scarcity of labor, particularly at the low income end, forcing employers to pay more. Philip Cafaro, whose book I referenced earlier, presents lots of evidence that illegal immigration has depressed wages in construction and meat packing.

3. Environmental sustainability supposedly requires a shrinking population. I list this argument despite vehemently disagreeing with it. Cafaro seems to think the US might serve as a beacon of beautiful environment by shrinking its population. I argue in my chapter on global warming that the right answer is technology and a more powerful United States, not a shrunken one. In any case, global population is likely

---

57 Harvard-Harris poll, January 2018, showing 81% of Americans want a reduction in immigration. The poll also showed Americans prefer (79% to 21%) more immigration be education and skill based rather than family-reunification based.

to shrink due to higher education and GDP growth, not the opposite. As countries' GDP and education grow, their birth rates shrink.

Here are some of the key reasons to support higher immigration, or at least maintenance of the current level:

1. The bigger the US economy, the better. A bigger economy means more power to maintain democratic values globally, more power to solve global warming and other global problems, lower taxes per person to support the same military, and a stronger defense against the authoritarian regimes that threaten global peace.

2. Without immigration the US population would shrink, reducing US influence in the world, and creating an ever heavier burden on US workers to foot the bill for our growing senior population. We actually need immigrants to prevent long term collapse. The current level of a million or so a year may sound large, but it's just 0.3% of the population, and barely adequate to keep us stable.

3. We have a moral responsibility to love our neighbors, to help the world's wretched poor, and to offer refuge to the oppressed. We can't and needn't take all of them, but compared to other countries, the US ranks pretty low. We should be better.

12: ONE PERSON ONE VOTE

On average, mailed-in ballots have about the same split between Republican and Democrat votes as in-person ballots. Even in 2020's bitterly contested election, with charges that mail-in ballots would fraudulently decide the presidency, a Stanford University study found that voting by mail did not preferentially help the Democrats[58].

So both parties should support greater ability to vote by mail, on the principle of increased democracy: the right to vote.

Many Republicans, encouraged by Fox News and other right wing media, are sincerely concerned about voter fraud, and support laws making it harder to vote, to make sure nobody votes who shouldn't, and that nobody gets to vote twice. In the United States, democracy matters a lot, and voter

---

58 "Study: Voting by mail did not help Dems" Associate Press article published in the Milwaukee Journal Sentinel Mar 7, 2021. Among other examples, the study looked at Texas, where mail-in voting was not changed for the pandemic. 65-year-old Texans can vote by mail without challenge. The difference in Republican vs. Democrat votes for 64 vs. 65 year olds was 0.2%.

fraud is very thoroughly investigated. So far, the number of cases of voter fraud detected are outgunned by the number of people dying from lightning strikes (which is about 27 people per year in the US). On the other hand, the number of American citizens prevented from voting through tough voter ID laws and other voter-suppression techniques is in the millions, and growing with each election.

Let's get serious about reducing voter fraud, since so many Americans worry about it, and put in place a system that very strongly enforces one person one vote. Let's have an identification system in America that makes extremely clear who each person is, and what their citizenship and voting status is. Technology has made this possible. Every single human being in the United States can be identified, so that every single one with the right to vote can do so easily.

I recognize some Americans fear and loathe the idea of government knowing more (or anything) about them, so this system would have to be carefully protected against unauthorized use. I would build it on top of systems that are already in place. Start with your Social Security Number (SSN), which Americans already do their best to protect, and make it even safer. Let's assign one to every human being who enters the US, by birth or plane or boat or train or car or bike or foot, and require a DNA sample, fingerprints, and retinal scan to associate with it. Give every American a photo ID linked to their SSN. Include a code and password, like your average bank card, to reduce identity theft. Require that identification verifying it's you, for key activities:

— Entering the United States

— Registering a birth

— Registering at a school or university

— Getting a job

— Opening a bank account (and absolutely all government payments, from welfare to social security, should be done only to a bank account clearly linked with the owner's SSN)

— Getting a phone

— Filing taxes

— Voting

The amount of verification can depend on the sensitivity of the transaction, maybe just giving your password to get a report on your tax return, but a retinal scan to cast your ballot.

On earlier drafts a friend warned me Democrats might see such tough voter identification as voter suppression. It would be, if the new ID card was hard to get, or required for voting before every American could get one. Those are solvable problems. India's similar program reached over 500 million people in 5 years. Note the US population including children is just 332 million.

I suggest the rollout be rigorous but rapid, a major government investment in the integrity of elections, with huge benefits in crime reduction.

Some illegal entries may fraudulently slip through, and even find cash work, but this would make unauthorized residency, tax dodging, money laundering, and illegal voting all extremely difficult.

One person one vote is an ideal increasingly damaged by the evolution of American election management. Gerrymandering, voter suppression, foreign interference, massive spending, and obsolete census data are making the US less democratic every election, creating resentment and disenfranchisement. Like other democratic countries, America should put all its voting in independent rather than political hands, with electoral districts created roughly contiguous, with roughly equal numbers of voters, by an agency monitored by both parties to ensure neutrality. Fraud should be seriously investigated, but the reality is that the only significant voter fraud in the US today is the gerrymandering and voter suppression which give a party control with far less than the popular vote.

I wish we could cap election spending per candidate, PACs included, at some amount that prevents money being a major driver in who gets elected, but the courts have decided that unlimited campaign spending is a form of free speech. But at least all political advertisements should state who is funding them - true for television today but not Internet postings. All political ads must be available for all to see - unlike targeted social media ads today. This caveat to free speech is justified by the current drowning out of less funded speakers, as well as the demand for one person one vote, as opposed to one thousand dollars one vote.

This issue is one of the toughest in this book, for me to hope for Republican support, but let me try.

Republicans can win. The US is a conservative country — Nixon and Reagan won by landslides. Even George Bush junior, who oversaw the intelligence organizations that let 9-11 happen, launched a war on nonexistent Iraqi weapons of mass destruction, and dramatically increased the federal deficit, won re-election by a large majority of the popular vote. When the Republican Party puts forward a decent leader and a great platform, they win easily. They sometimes win even with a terrible candidate. There is no need to prevent blacks or young people or Latinos from voting, except when the Republican Party is operating out of fear, with a losing platform and a losing leader.

Not every politician in the US works very hard to get every American a vote. This brings shame to principled conservatives who believe in democracy. In the long run, I believe conservatives will put forward winning platforms and winning candidates, with no need to pervert democracy to win power. Increasingly, though slowly, states are changing their laws to avoid gerrymandering, and to allocate electoral college votes by their popular vote. This will improve American democracy, and give both parties an equal chance to win, based on the visions they put forward, instead of the votes they prevent, or the votes they buy.

13: ALLIES AND ENEMIES

The fraught global economy and politics require wise action to protect American interests. Trump's practice of treating friends like enemies (Canada, Mexico, Europe, Japan), and dictators like "dear friends" (Vladimir Putin, Kim Jong Un, Salman bin Abdulaziz Al Saud) did not help the progress of human rights globally, and damaged the US and global economy, but Trump was not typical of American foreign policy. The world's poor, in rights and in standard of living, can be served by multilateral trade improvements, and muscular US-led intervention in selective cases to prevent the worst crimes against humanity. Specifically, the World Trade Organization needs to be staffed and strengthened to stand up to China and other trade bullies, rather than weakened and sidelined. Coalitions should be built, as Bush senior did, to combat the worst terrorists. Iran's march toward a nuclear bomb, restored and accelerated by Trump's abandonment of the treaty which stopped it, should be renegotiated. The nuclear disarmament treaties with Russia and all other nations should be extended and strengthened. More free trade, particularly with poor nations, to stimulate their economies, will lower prices across the world, and increase all standards of living, except the very small percentage of rich world populations which currently live on high-priced subsidized agriculture.

Firm negotiations, sanctions, and other ongoing pressure should be applied to all countries which deny the human rights agreed by the United Nations. Here Trump's administration actually outperformed previous presidents, levying more sanctions on transgressing leaders. This particularly includes the regimes of Iran, Syria, North Korea, China, and Russia. When those countries are more free, not only will humanity be better off, but the increased global economy will mean greater markets and resources for America.

China is a special case, as the only other superpower on Earth. China does not honor the spirit of the WTO or the Universal Declaration of Human Rights. Its trade practices are unfair, keeping out foreign competition while benefiting from access to global markets. China also threatens to subjugate Taiwan as it has Hong Kong, and large swathes of the South China Sea, further removing rights from additional people. If China were a firm supporter of human rights, its rise as a global power could be welcomed, but under Xi Jinping, China has moved further toward self-serving autocracy, and away from benevolent technocracy, hence even further from the ideal of democracy (or communism, for that matter)

US policy toward such a China should be friendly but firm, not allowing China to unfairly profit through weakness of the democratic world, but constantly engaging to attempt negotiated solutions, issue by issue. In this the US should coordinate with all democratic nations to present unified pressure. Strengthen the WTO and use it to resolve trade disputes. Build the US Navy's role in the Pacific to guarantee the safety and rights of allies including Taiwan, Japan, South Korea, and all of Southeast Asia. Create a NATO equivalent for the Pacific. Slowly but steadily pressure the Chinese government to support human rights, starting with sanctions targeting the most egregious violations such as those against Uighurs in Xinjiang.

While the above will likely make China-US relations even more strained, working together on common goals should help make them more friendly. China and the US have common cause in repairing global warming, restoring the health of global oceans, fighting pandemics, and preventing North Korea from acting irresponsibly.

This book centers on recommended policies for the United States, where I live. But while I am dispensing unsolicited advice for one superpower, why not for the other as well? I love China, having traveled there several times on business and on vacation. I have visited five of China's provinces, its three biggest cities, and some of its more remote parks. For years I have studied Chinese language, practiced Chinese martial arts, and made countless Chinese friends. Of course the Chinese people have the right to define their own path, but here is a possible path I see, which I believe would lead China to become the world's greatest power, and the Chinese Communist Party the most powerful and respected force on Earth:

1. Chairman Xi Jinping retire now that he has served over ten years, in accordance with the post-Mao tradition.

2. Establish freedom of religion, particularly for Uighurs and Tibetan Buddhists, welcoming the Dalai Lama back to Tibet as leader of his religion, while perhaps requiring that all Party members be declared atheists, to keep religion out of politics and out of government.

3. Restore Hong Kong to its "one country two systems" state of some years ago, and allowing development there of a full multi-party democracy.

4. Continue to substantially grow Chinese military capability, to become a peer to the United States.

5. Declare Taiwan a separate and fully sovereign state, while welcoming a unification with China in future, should Taiwan hold a free and fair referendum choosing unification. Withdraw the stick and rely entirely on the carrot.

6. Negotiate disputed borders with all its neighbors, including maritime claims, with an extreme generosity, handing over the South China Sea, and the bulk of disputed islands and border regions to India, Japan, Vietnam, and others. China's magnanimity would raise its global status, and cost almost nothing economically or militarily, particularly as China's military capability grows.

7. Apply its military force to combat piracy and terrorism, working constructively with the US military, to forge partnerships in global trouble spots, to get to know each other better, and build communication pathways that will safeguard peace between them.

8. Actively work on denuclearizing all countries on Earth, starting particularly with the rogue states Iran and North Korea.

9. Immediately halt all construction of coal power plants by Chinese organizations worldwide, as part of efforts to turn around global warming, while continuing work on green energy.

10. Uphold the spirit and letter of World Trade Organization agreements, to foster truly free global markets for goods and services, inviting foreign competition into China.

With these ten actions, I think China would rapidly come to rival the United States as the place wherever most people on Earth would go and live if they could. I think Taiwan might welcome unification then. While I hope China embarks on a peaceful rise something like the above, I am not naïve enough to count on it. Therefore I believe in a muscular foreign policy for the US, with the following pillars:

- The US should continue to clearly articulate, repeatedly and in all forums, its foreign interests, which should boil down to America's values, which it shares with human beings around the world: democracy, free press, independent judiciary, rule of law, freedom of speech.

- To countries that uphold the same values, the US should extend many benefits, including increasingly free trade, and mutual defense guarantees (that is, the extension of NATO to democracies worldwide).

- To countries that denigrate or threaten those values, the US should extend a hand of friendship, of hope and promise that mutual understanding can lead to ever better relationships — but measured, continually increasing pressures should the offers be declined.

- Among those actions, the US should establish a constant and significant naval presence in the South China Sea, equal to the Chinese presence, declining in proportion to Chinese withdrawal, or Chinese moves toward democracy, and increasing if China continues to increase its construction there.

14: FOREIGN AID

The US spends about $35 billion per year on foreign aid, #1 in absolute terms. As a percentage of GDP, the US is at about 0.1% of GDP, similar to the generosity of Greece, Slovenia, and Korea. The world leader is Sweden at about 1% of GDP, that is about 10 times as much as the US!

That foreign aid rescues human beings from starvation, epidemics, and poverty. When spent intelligently, it leads to real human progress, permanent improvements in the standard of living in benighted countries[59].

My policy on foreign aid might be political poison, but I will stand on my principles, and put it forward anyway. I believe the best way to stimulate human progress in poor countries is to buy more from them. Incrementally, to the

---

[59] Read page 95 of Pinker's "Enlightenment Now" for a wealth of references and stories to overcome the bad rap of foreign aid, and regain some optimism about the amazing increases in the quality of life in supposed African basket cases.

extent that those countries support human rights (democracy, freedom of speech, free press, etc.) we should remove trade barriers and encourage Americans to find terrific value in buying from them. What would we buy? I would like the free market to decide that. Probably America and American companies would buy lots of cheap food, and cheap labor.

Why is this political poison? Because I am talking about making our market more free, letting poor people from Africa or South America or anywhere that democracy is blooming sell to America. Today, we impose huge tariffs to prevent poor farmers in those countries from competing with American farmers. We impose tariffs to prevent cheap labor from working in the US, or manufacturing things for us. If we reduce those tariffs, Americans overall will get a boosted standard of living, as we can buy the same food and goods and services for cheaper, but some protected parts of American industry will fall to the competition. Farmers are an extremely strong lobby group in the US, and a significant 11% of all US employment, even more than manufacturing, which is about 9%. Both of these will suffer if we give poor countries a level playing field to compete with us, and so the politicians will suffer who try to level the field, even just a little bit, to help the poorest countries. Is there a way to get the benefits for all Americans, and for those poor countries, without that backlash? I have a few suggestions:

1. Buy land from failing farms. Reducing tariffs from poor democracies is motivated by the goals of foreign aid, and the improvement to American living standards by finding cheaper supply chains. This is worth spending some government money on. That can be spent, instead of the current $20 billion or so per year that subsidizes American agriculture, to buy out farmers' lands if they want to sell, at high prices. The land can go to parks, or non-agricultural development, depending where it lies.

2. Hiring agricultural staff to support the import effort. American experts will be needed to train overseas farmers, to monitor the quality of imports, and to invest in import businesses.

3. Most important, do not dismantle US agriculture. The strongest and best American producers will continue to out-compete any farmers anywhere, particularly to serve their local markets. High quality fresh organic foods, for example, are most efficiently sourced locally, as a free market will continue to show. Change to tariffs should be gradual, announced with plenty of time for industry to make sound investments and other decisions. Access to the US market should be measured, withheld or reduced for abuses of American interests, and small enough that no industry is traumatized with sudden massive job losses.

This does not mean zero job loss or zero transformation of the US. Over the past 100 years, agriculture has declined from about 8 million to 2 million jobs while the overall population has tripled. US manufacturing over the last 100 years has dropped in half as a fraction of total employment. And yet, unemployment in the US, just prior to Covid-19's attack, was at historic lows. Americans have found new ways to work, new ways to make money, steadily improving themselves, as the world changed.

15: SOCIAL SECURITY AND UBI

A time bomb of underfunded social security is ticking. Without changes to its provisions, or the tax system, given our aging society, social security will be bankrupt by 2035, starting with having paid out more than it takes in since 2020. Opinion of some radical thinker? No, this is from the April 2019 annual report to Congress by the Board of Trustees who oversee Social Security[60].

Intelligent politicians on both sides of the aisle are well aware of the problem, but the US political climate has not allowed them to cooperate on a solution. Some other countries have faced and solved the same challenge. Canada solved it, for example, without changing the terms of its social security equivalent, by increasing payroll taxes, to bring in the right amount of money to provide the promised service, assuming competitive investment returns, and putting the funds under control of an arms-length investment board. US pension funds

---

[60] www.ssa.gov/oact/TR/

assume investment returns of 10% or even 15%, and hence are drastically underfunded. Social Security doesn't even put the funds in a bank; the money goes out as it comes in. In this chapter, I advocate ideas to fix Social Security without raising taxes, and without cutting benefits for retired Americans.

I explored a popular idea in my novel, **Control Theory: A Science Fiction Love Story**. I believe that in the future, all governments on Earth will send every one of their citizens a regular Universal Basic Income (UBI). In the novel I called it "the Stipend" and fantasized it would start in Europe around 2022. Ironically, as I first wrote this in 2020, Andrew Yang made a $1000 monthly UBI a major plank of his bid to become president, and the US government considered launching this exact idea as an emergency response to the Covid pandemic. The federal government under both Trump and Biden indeed sent multiple stimulus payments to every American resident (except the top few %), to get the country through the wave of unemployment and bankruptcies of the pandemic. Just as an $800 billion government package prevented the banks from going bankrupt in 2009 (which would have meant all your bank accounts suddenly had no money in them), this similar-sized package helped stop the economy from grinding to a halt. People who needed it spent their stimulus checks on each other, getting food and shelter and everything else. This helped keep the businesses that provide those necessities alive, and incidentally wiped out much of US child poverty for two years.

Outside of a crisis like Covid-19, a UBI starting at an affordable level would have lots of other benefits for society. The idea has been around for a long time, though it gained awareness through the 2020 Democratic Primaries, and even more with Covid. It has been trialed in small communities, with measurable success[61], including savings for government.

---

61 See "Cheques and Balances" in The Economist, March 6, 2021 for an overview of growing support and evidence for UBI.

For example, in a Swedish study recipients of a UBI were more likely, not less, to obtain work. How could giving everyone money save money? By replacing the complicated bureaucratic mess of a hundred different welfare programs by a single, simple money transfer.

I would consolidate Social Security, along with unemployment insurance, welfare programs, and virtually all other federal government programs for the poor, into a single universal basic income (UBI) for every citizen of the US, clawed back in taxes from the most wealthy. The federal government would do a weekly transfer into every citizen's bank account who does not have high income. As income rises, the federal transfer would decline, so there is always a benefit to working, but everyone gets a minimum income. I would initially make the amount "revenue neutral", so this is not an increase of welfare spending, just a more efficient method. As the country gets wealthier, we would gradually increase that minimum income until it supports what we collectively consider the minimum standard of living we allow in a civilized country.

There are many reasons for a UBI. One is to control inflation. Until 2022, inflation had collapsed in all the advanced economies. Most economists and rich-world central banks believe inflation of about 2% is ideal, and healthy, but all their tools had failed to get inflation up to this level. It's ironic for those of us who remember the 1970s, when inflation was too high instead of too low. I remember expecting at least 10% raises every year just to keep up with inflation. People planned on 5-10% inflation. The Fed fixed that, with echos around the world, as they raised interest rates high enough to kill inflation. Unfortunately they overshot. Japan's economy has been suffering from deflation for decades. Their stock market had yet to recover its 1989 peak, 30 years later. During the 2008 financial crisis, the Fed was worried about collapsing liquidity — in other words, about not enough money to keep the economy going, which would lead to collapsing prices, the opposite of inflation. What tool did they use to save the world?

Quantitative Easing (QE). Many amateur economists and conservative politicians who don't understand finance thought they were crazy. The Fed at the peak of the financial crisis spent $40 billion every month creating new money. Did it cause massive inflation as feared? Or did it work as expected? It did not work as well as hoped, because the US economy took years to get back to the same level, and inflation stayed stuck well below 2%, but it worked well enough. The US did not enter another Great Depression. After a few years, the stock market and the economy were back to peak levels.

What might have worked better than interest rates and QE, to control inflation to healthy levels? Let's analyze what happened to that $40 billion per month the Fed created. Remember the intent was to put more money into the US economy, so businesses could rebuild, consumers could spend, and everything would get cooking again. Inflation of 2% is a great way to know that the economy is cooking at just the right speed. It's a bit like keeping a pot simmering on the stove. If it's boiling over (10% inflation) you know the heat is too high. If it stops boiling at all (less than 2% inflation) you need to turn up the heat. During and after QE, inflation stayed well below 2%. I believe the reason was the chosen mechanism for distributing the $40 billion per month. Constrained by federal law, the Fed's only option at the time was to buy US Treasury Bonds. In theory, this money would trickle down through the economy. Buying government bonds would reduce interest rates overall, so companies could easily borrow more money, which would let companies do more innovation, and spending would rise to consume it. That is not what happened. The Fed created all that money, and bought the bonds from the mostly rich people and corporations that had them. The top 1% got even richer. Companies piled up even more cash. Interest rates did drop, and companies did borrow more... but they did not spend the money on more innovation. Instead, they largely spent the money on buybacks to increase share prices. It's a good thing not a bad thing if the stock market rises, but QE led to the top 1% getting richer, while underachieving its original intent.

I believe a better way to implement QE, whenever it is needed, is to give the money directly and evenly to everyone in the country. Instead of trying to get an indirect effect through lowering interest rates, this instantly creates more demand. Rich bond holders who suddenly get $100,000 more cash do not typically go out and spend it, while the average person who gets $1,000 more cash will spend most of it. That spending drives the economy, with companies working hard and innovating to be the recipient of that spending. The amazingly fast recovery of the US economy after the Covid spike is evidence of that. It works both ways: tuning a UBI up or down would affect inflation much faster than the current tools of interest rate changes and bond purchases.

The 2009 QE of $40 billion per month, divided by about 325 million people in the US, would be $123 per person, including children, per month. In 2021 as I wrote this paragraph, the Fed's QE was running at $120 billion per month, or $369 per person, to fight the economic crisis caused by the corona virus. It was being done in a more complex way: governments were sending out checks to everyone in the country, and the central bank was buying government bonds at the same time, covering the growth in government debt. I suggest cutting the politicians out of the loop, and giving the Fed a permanent mandate to distribute cash to everyone in the country, with a goal of 2% inflation. The amount may be very small or zero when the economy is cooking on its own, but when a cold snap comes in, the Fed can add heat by adjusting the amount as needed.

I suggest legislating to authorize the Federal Reserve to supplement the government UBI with created money, as an alternative to bond purchases and other monetary methods. It would be up to the Fed how best to achieve its goals of 2% inflation and minimum unemployment (no change from today), but it would have an additional tool to consider. As interest rates and unemployment have dropped to historically low levels, and inflation has flipped from far below the Fed's goal to far above, quantitative easing through bond purchases has not been as effective as hoped. Direct cash transfers to the country's poorest, to stimulate demand, would likely be far more effective. The amount can be small, to be modified over time by the Fed in response to inflation trends, to keep the financial system stable.

Note this Fed supplement is meant as an addendum to the main UBI, which can be funded without any tax increases. Only one of my proposals in this book costs extra money not spent by government today, and it's not this one. See the diagram below, with actual 2019 spending on the left, and proposed UBI on the right.

Figure 1: Government Spending 2019 vs. Proposal*

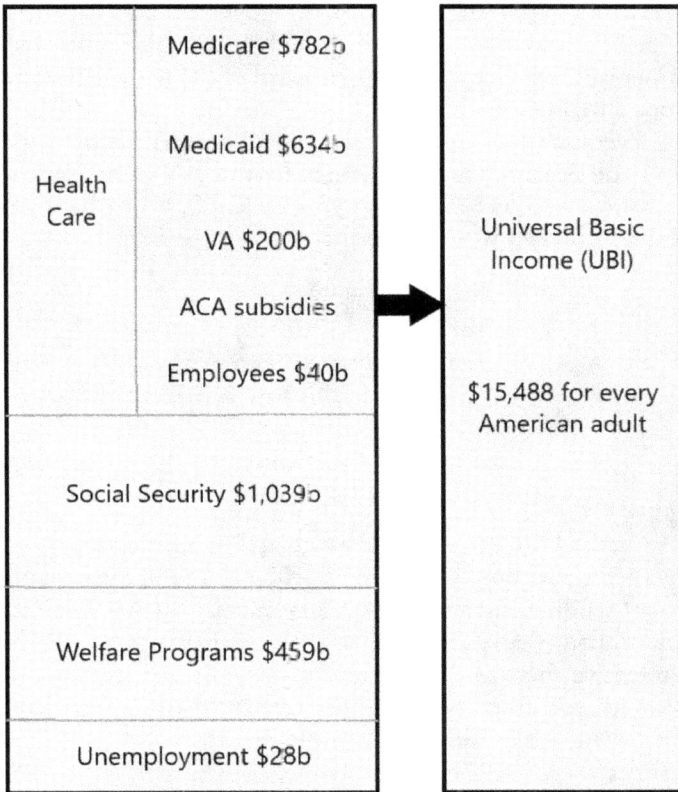

Health Care	Medicare $782b	Universal Basic Income (UBI)
	Medicaid $634b	
	VA $200b	
	ACA subsidies	
	Employees $40b	$15,488 for every American adult
Social Security $1,039b		
Welfare Programs $459b		
Unemployment $28b		

* "b" is for billions. Medicaid and Welfare include state as well as federal spending. Total $3,237 billion, which works out to $15,488 for each of 209 million American adults, per year.

Would we really be better off, giving every American adult $15,488 per year, instead of spending those taxes the way we currently are, on welfare and unemployment, social security and Medicare, Medicaid and the VA? This would be a radical change. It would make some people poorer, and others richer. It would save an enormous amount of bureaucratic overhead, and hence shrink the size of the US government. That should appeal to conservatives. It would also make sure every American has a basic, decent standard of living, which should appeal to liberals.

Everyone who can work would still be strongly motivated to work, because they will benefit enormously from doing so. Imagine living on $15,844 per year back in 2019. Perhaps your monthly budget would be as follows:

- $700 rent for a studio apartment
- $300 food
- $200 health insurance (except this isn't enough, which I address in the Health Care chapter as well as later in this chapter)
- $91 left over for everything else: cellphone, utilities, hair cuts, clothing

On the UBI alone, you're surviving but not thriving. If you can get a part time job paying $1300 per month, you double your spending budget, since taxes would eat barely 10% at that low income level. Unlike welfare, where you have an alternative between working for peanuts, or getting free peanuts, this keeps everyone motivated to earn what they can. I believe this will eliminate the welfare trap.

Yes there will be some people who blow their UBI on drugs, or become so lazy they just scrape by on the UBI and don't bother to work. Keep the UBI low enough, and I believe there is sufficient motivation that almost everyone who can work will work.

Search Google for UBI and you will find approximately 110,000 entries. There has been a lot of press and research. Studies contradict each other. Some found terrific savings to government and much happier citizens, while others found no benefit at all. For the American Plan I propose, here are some key benefits, which I think will prove themselves within a few months of implementation:

- This is designed to be revenue neutral. Exactly the same amount of government tax revenue gets spent as before, but with a much simpler model. Over time, this means government can make its workforce leaner, and get the same benefit for fewer dollars. The plan doesn't depend on laying off government workers, but it allows for it, if they're no longer needed.

- Fewer people will fall through the cracks. Today, there are too many stories of the hard worker who doesn't quite make enough to afford health care, and the single mother who can't find work but used up her welfare allowance for her state, or the mentally ill homeless person who gets nothing. Instead of yet another government program to try to catch a hundred categories of people who need help, this gives every American a basis to live.

- This gets government out of the insurance business. Unemployment Insurance is one of the eliminated programs. No more bureaucracy to decide who does and doesn't get a payment. If anyone wants insurance that their income will be higher than the UBI, in case they lose their job, there is a free market for insurance. They or their employer could buy supplementary policies.

Let's look at the winners and losers if we simply switched the taps as shown in Figure 1, and adjust the plans to make it work better.

First, better off Americans don't need an extra $15,488 per year. They'd love to have it, of course, but let's steer that money where it's needed. In 2019, the year of the spending totals shown above, over 72 million Americans filed taxes for income higher than 100,000. We don't have to raise their net taxes any higher, just raise them enough to tax back that $15,488. That would give us about $1.1 trillion to spend on rebalancing, that is $1,100 billion.

Current recipients of Social Security are entitled to their current benefits. Those averaged out in 2019 to $17,652 per year, a bit higher than the proposed UBI. We could provide a Social Security supplement to make them whole, for a total cost of $136 billion.

The proposed UBI is for adults. Some of the tax savings should go to top up the UBI for children. This should go to the custodial parent, in case of split households, replacing all cash-disbursing welfare programs.

My estimate for health care was $200 per month. Unfortunately the real cost of health care in the US today is about $1000 per person per month. See my chapter on health care for how this can be competed down to a lower cost, but in the short run, it will require a bump-up to the UBI for poor people, and a balancing claw-back for rich people, to make this work.

Depending on your definition, this may or may not eliminate poverty. In today's dollars, this UBI is below the poverty level by several official definitions, but I've lived on less myself, and believe it's a decent basis. For those who receive such a UBI and still find themselves homeless, or begging, or drifting to crime, I don't believe the answer should be more government handouts, but rather increased effort on social work, education, mental health, and coaching.

I think this approach to an American UBI should appeal to both conservatives and liberals. For the same government spending, or somewhat less when the bureaucracy is slimmed down, we'll have no American without health care, no beggars on the streets, no homelessness, and no poverty.

The American government, without raising taxes, could balance its Social Security books by raising the retirement age automatically in line with longevity, combining the benefit with the universal basic income (UBI), and clawing the benefit back for high-income citizens who don't need it. Let me address a couple impassioned arguments against this idea: one, that we've been paying into social security so we deserve the payout when we retire, and two, "if you touch my social security I won't vote for you." These two points have led to both parties of Congress keeping their heads firmly planted in the sand, unwilling to touch the looming problem.

The first argument doesn't stand rational investigation. Unfortunately, Social Security was never designed as a retirement savings program. It is fundamentally structured to "pay as you go" since its creation in 1935. It started small, but even the first recipient, Ernest Ackerman of Cleveland Ohio, got more than he paid for. Ernest received a lump sum payment of 17 cents, having retired after just one paycheck with Social Security taxes charged. He had paid in 5 cents. Social Security does not take your taxes and save them up to pay you on retirement. It pays current retirees out of the taxes paid by current workers. Most years there has been a surplus, but the total surplus since 1935 would barely cover one year of payouts. The best you can ask of such a program if you are paying into it today is that future workers pay for your retirement, just as you are paying current retirees. But if there are more retirees than workers, twenty years from now, as forecast, this won't work. You have no moral position to require future workers to pay far higher taxes than you do, to pay you the same social security. It is more accurate for you to think of the Social Security tax as just another part of your income tax, which goes to fund various government programs for the year you are paying it.

The second argument is harder to tackle. Retired voters, and voters thinking about their retirement, understandably want to maximize the money they get, and will punish politicians who threaten to reduce it, or to raise taxes to pay for it. Much easier to just defer the problem to future politicians. This is a political calculus. Perhaps it will be best just to leave the Social Security problem alone for another 10-15 years, when it becomes an immediate financial crisis, rather than trying to solve it now, but this book is about offering solutions that can fly now, so let's try.

If a political leader believes Social Security should be

repaired, in the way this book proposes, here are the arguments they can make to a skeptical public:

1. The new method, based on a UBI, will pay the majority of Americans the same amount as they would have got on Social Security. The rich will get less. The very poor will be helped out more.

2. The US Government should not be in the mutual fund business. Let's not have the government compete with the free market for retirement planning or investment. Leave it to the market. More socialist countries, like Canada, can set up a national retirement savings plan for everyone, but that's not the American way.

3. If we do not act, Social Security will bankrupt the government by the time most of today's working population gets old enough to collect it. It is simply too generous, as currently designed, for the demographics of the second half of this century.

4. Nevertheless, for people who are worried, we will grandfather into the UBI legislation that replaces Social Security, that everyone over 40 at the time of passage, who can be assumed to have legitimately counted on Social Security in their retirement planning, will get a top-up to their UBI to match what they would have got on Social Security. In most cases there won't be any top-up needed, and it should be eliminated for people over a certain "rich" income threshold.

401K Reform

Since we are discussing government's role in retirement planning, let's improve the 401K and related tax incentives. When I moved to the US from Canada some years ago, I was surprised to learn that the American retirement planning system has more in common with Communist China than it does with Canada's free market system. "Surprised" is an understatement. I was shocked and dismayed. Just like in the old days of Communist China, in the US, your employer decides what kind of retirement savings options you have. Your employer makes a deal with a 401k provider, and that provider offers a limited set of their own mutual funds, and perhaps one or two other vehicles, like stock in your employer, for you to buy. If you are not employed by a company large enough to offer a 401k program, you are limited to a much lower contribution to an IRA.

My American friends might be interested in the Canadian system, called a Registered Retirement Savings Plan (RRSP). The RRSP has the same tax treatment as an American 401k. It has similar annual contribution limits, and similar withdrawal rules when you retire. The big difference is that any Canadian can buy any RRSP in the country. It is not tied to any particular employer. Most RRSPs allow you to invest in a huge range of things, from stocks to bonds to mutual funds to ETFs. Some are fully managed, for a fee, and some let you trade your own stocks. Canadian financial institutions compete hard to win peoples' RRSP business, unlike the near-monopolies in the US, where companies rarely change 401k providers. To me, the US system looks like a racket.

My last employer in Canada, like most Canadian companies, offered to match my RRSP contribution, just as American companies often match 401k contributions.

I urge the US to convert to the Canadian system, outlaw the monopolization of 401k plans by a single provider for each employer. This would stimulate healthy competition to improve the options and performance of everyone's retirement accounts.

16: RACISM AND CRT

George Floyd was a man of extremes, of transformation. He's known to have said, often, that he was going to change the world, and perhaps he did.

Earlier in his life, Mr. Floyd did some horrible things, including rape and robbery. He was convicted of eight crimes from 1997 to 2005, and spent four years in prison. Then, like America is good at, he changed. In his new home of Minneapolis, he became known as a gentle giant, a night club bouncer loved by the patrons, because he was kind and careful[62].

I wrote the first version of this book in the Spring and Summer of 2020. Fear of Covid-19 kept me off the streets, but many of my friends joined the Black Lives Matter (BLM) protests. It's tragic that the movement's popularity had to be based on a series of race-based deaths, but I find joy and hope in the swelling of support for Black Lives Matter, the large numbers of people of all races all over the world who joined.

Yes, the US has suffered from horrible discrimination, and continues to suffer from race conflict, but racism continues to decline steadily[63]. As I wrote this sentence, millions of Americans were on the streets protesting against the conditions that led to Floyd's death. These millions included every race, every age, every socioeconomic class, and very

---

[62] "Who was George Floyd? The 'gentle giant' who was trying to turn his life around. Sky News, June 7, 2020.
[63] See the Equal Rights chapter of Pinker's "Englightenment Now" for a host of related statistics.

importantly, every political party. Back in 2010, 51% of Americans saw racial discrimination as a big problem in the US[64], and after George Floyd, it rose to 76%, which means the believers included both parties, and all classes. More of us are trying to understand what "Black Lives Matter" means and why it's important, and I don't think it's naïvely optimistic to predict that racism will continue to be significantly beaten back, over the coming years. This is a country that can change, and does continually change, with remarkable progress. The country of Lincoln will not rest until the legacy of slavery is eradicated. Optimists claim it already is, and pessimists say it never will be, but either way, I see a country continually improving.

Indeed the most common conservative positions in the US today do not try to defend racism, but rather claim racism is over, and affirmative action is no longer needed. Isn't it wonderful that we're no longer trying to remove racist laws, but instead worrying about how much legal effort to put into counterbalancing past racism? Of all forms of discrimination that still poison America, I think anti-black racism damages the most lives today, and hence my devotion of a full chapter to it. Even if you think like my forever Trump friend that affirmative action has gone too far and blacks are advantaged more than disadvantaged, I think you'll admit that race remains a big issue in America. But let's also celebrate the progress already made. Google for studies by Harvard, the University of Illinois' Institute of Government and Public Affairs, or almost any other quantitative source, and you can see racism and racist attitudes decline steadily over time[65]. The question is whether they've moved far enough.

While "soft" measures such as the percentage of Americans

---

[64] The Economist (June 11, 2020)

[65] For example: "Patterns of implicit and explicit attitudes: Long-term change and stability from 2007 to 2016" in Psychological Science...
https://journals.sagepub.com/doi/abs/10.1177/0956797618813087?journalCode=pssa

supporting BLM rise, harder measures like the wage gap between black and white Americans have stayed stubbornly lopsided for decades[66]. I think the best answer, the best action, is to improve poor schools. When American black children overall get the same quality of education as American white children, I believe they will attain the same salaries, the same positions, the same full enjoyment of rights as their white compatriots. Yes there is still work to do on the minority of Americans who practice racist discrimination, but the biggest improvement in black lives will come from investing in equality of education.

Efforts to desegregate schools, and give promising black children more opportunities in higher education, do help, but for the vast majority of poor black children, the poor quality of their schools condemns them to always being behind their richer white brother and sister Americans. This is because America funds its schools primarily out of local property taxes, which means poor communities get poor schools, and rich communities get rich schools.

Canada scores quite a bit higher than the US on the PISA tests of 15 year olds around the world, despite Canada spending quite a bit less on K-12 education. Canada's provinces range from about $9000 per pupil to $12,000, a difference large enough to generate media articles calling it scandalous. Those are Canadian dollars, now worth about 75 cents US. The US varies from about $8000 in Idaho to $25,000 in New York, and the range within a single state (Wisconsin, for example) goes as high as 2.5 from best to worst funded[67], even after all government attempts at equalization.

This is the one area I believe the US federal government

[66] "Report: State of Black America looks grim" by Michael Warren, Associated Press, April 13, 2022. Dramatic differences in mortgage approval, longevity, wealth, maternal mortality, suicide, and homicide.
[67] https://www.jsonline.com/story/opinion/2022/09/07/make-wisconsins-school-funding-system-equitable-all-districts/7976076001/

needs to step in with more investment. Every other adjustment to federal spending in this book is revenue-neutral — I've designed all the policies to cost the same or less than what the government spends today. After all, I may be socially liberal but I'm financially conservative, like most Canadians. But the abysmal quality and low budgets of the average American elementary and high school is a disgrace, and a drag on the American economy.

My proposal for fixing schools is in another chapter, but I want to repeat the core ideas here, because it's the best way I see to make black lives better in this country. We should establish a level of funding and quality we believe is "good enough" for the best country in the world, and make that the minimum for every school in the land. That will be expensive, but it will be worth it.

Sadly, even if we bring every school in America up to some minimal standard, and even if we did it in an amazingly short 3-4 years, this will take a generation to complete, and won't much help the tens of millions of adult Americans who went through the current low-quality bottom half of our system. What most needs doing to give all Americans equal opportunity, when so many have been pushed down their whole lives?

Should we design a program of reparations to counterbalance the systemic racism of previous generations? The idea of reparations exploded for a while after the George Floyd protests, but remains unpopular among Americans – one poll found it rose from 23% to 39% from 2019 to 2020, among white people[68]. There is a precedent, in the $20,000 reparations paid to Japanese Americans interred during World War II. Before reparations can address black injustice, however, they would need to be designed to meet several difficult criteria: to be affordable for America, to be beneficial

---

68 "A national debt?", in the Milwaukee Journal Sentinel, Sep 12, 2021, written under an investigative journalism project of the University of Wisconsin, Madison. The article analyzes the current state of the reparations idea.

for America's economy overall, and to be popular enough to win support of over 50% of Americans. Even if it's a good idea, I don't think that will happen.

To be honest, I don't know well enough what the right answer is. I'm an incredibly lucky, privileged, white, middle-class male. I'm the wrong person to generate policy to fix the racial inequality of the US, so I know the first thing to do is a lot more listening and reading. I've been reading articles by black leaders, listening to my black friends, trying to learn.

What shocked me most, in the first months of that reading, was to learn how bad the inequality still is, for most blacks in America. For example, if you asked me what the difference in wealth was between the average white family, and the average black family, I would have said perhaps a 50% difference. It's closer to a 1000%, that is a factor 10. Wow. Thanks to BLM, I also discovered that black men across America learn to be very careful about entering white people's homes, even as invited guests. A black plumber will hesitate to do a house call in the evening, throughout the US, because the risk of being shot or otherwise assaulted, by the police or by "protective" neighbors, is too high. This needs more than better schools and a generation of slow progress to resolve.

This bring us to Critical Race Theory (CRT), another nexus in the polarized culture war between extremist conservatives and extremist liberals[69]. I was really puzzled by how much drama CRT creates in America. Why are people screaming and yelling in school board meetings about what books to ban? I tried to see both sides. I watched Tucker Carlson rant against CRT on Fox, and I watched John Oliver rant in defense of it.

---

[69]Cynical Theories: How Activist Scholarship Made Everything about Race, Gender, and Identity—and Why This Harms Everybody. By Helen Pluckrose and James Lindsay. I highly recommend this book for anyone who either hates or loves CRT, intersectionality, queer theory, or post-colonial theory. Not because it's right about everything, but because it presents a clear and thorough analysis of these theories and their impact on America. It combats the ignorance underlying most of this debate.

I suggest reading both "Critical Race Theory: An Introduction" by Richard Delgado, one of the founders and main proponents, as well as "Cynical Theories", by Pluckrose and Lindsay, who are heavily anti-CRT.

"I never figured out what CRT is, to be totally honest after a year talking about it. They're teaching that some races are inherently superior to others." That's Tucker Carlson saying he's criticizing something he doesn't understand, followed by a criticism of CRT which I know from actually studying it somewhat is blatantly false. Sadly, most of the vitriol about CRT is based on similar ignorance.

That doesn't mean CRT is correct, or that it should be taught in elementary school, but it irks me that so much book-banning is being done based on ignorance.

The core idea of CRT is twisted by some conservatives as "every white person is inherently racist". It's more accurate to say that CRT sees racial discrimination has been built into our systems over centuries. For example, no white man is decreeing that black kids in America should get inferior schools. Very few white Americans are explicitly racist like that anymore. However, minority kids on average are getting $2200 per year less school funding that white kids[70]. You can say this is nobody's fault, and certainly not the result of conscious racism. CRT says this is the subtle type of racism that still exists in our country, and that it should change. My progressive readers have no problem with this. My conservative readers are likely to disagree. If you disagree with the handful of facts I've listed here, I suggest you research them yourself. If you can convince yourself that the playing field is actually level in the US, or tilted in black people's favor, I question where you get your facts, but perhaps you can convince me. If you think government should just stay out of it, that anti-discrimination

---

[70] https://www.usnews.com/news/education-news/articles/2019-02-26/white-students-get-more-k-12-funding-than-students-of-color-report

laws in place today are enough, and black people should just work harder in the land of opportunity to come out on top, I respect your opinion. After all, Michelle Obama managed to get a Harvard Law degree despite growing up poor on the South Side of Chicago. This isn't the land of "everybody gets a free ride".

However, if we can come up with policies that help level that playing field, which also boost the overall economy, shouldn't even a conservative agree?

I have two suggestions in that vein. The first is a 1% of GDP boost to education I mentioned earlier. The US is behind most of the civilized world in its K-12 education. Improving the bottom half of our schools will help the country. Today we desperately import doctors and engineers because we can't grow enough of them at home. Let's grow more.

Thomas Sowell, a well known conservative, and incidentally black, Stanford professor noted in his book Economic Facts and Fallacies that the differences in American income between blacks and whites is fully explained by their differences in skills and education – that indeed blacks with the same education and measured intelligence had 6% higher income than whites, in one study. Another black writer, John McWhorter, in Woke Racism: How a New Religion has Betrayed Black America, also focuses his prescriptions for reducing America's race problems on education.

My second suggestion, also echoing McWhorter but with a twist, is to make it a federal crime to discriminate on the basis of paid debts to society. Today, it's routine for American organizations to do a criminal record check on all applicants. This hurts the economy by reducing job mobility. There are reasonable exceptions to make, such as keeping sexual predators away from children, and financial ex-cons away from other people's money, but in general, if a person has paid for their crime, it should not haunt them for life. Since a disproportionate number of ex-convicts are black, removing hiring discrimination based on previous convictions will help – their children, their grandchildren, and society as a whole.

Timothy Bult

17: CRIME

Is crime on the rise in America? Should we grow our police forces or shrink them? Should we put more people in prison for longer, or fewer for shorter? Should our prisons get more money or less? Should capital punishment be eliminated or increased?

Oddly again, like so many other questions, these are almost a non-issue in the rest of the civilized world, but a massive conflict in the US.

American prisons are ridiculously full and ineffective. Recidivism is high, as prisons are more schools for criminality than centers of rehabilitation. George Floyd's rehabilitation was sadly an exception rather than a rule. A criminal record is easily obtained in a country where smoking marijuana is a crime, and three minor thefts can lead to life in prison. An innocent person convicted of murder by a racist jury can be killed by the state, or spend twenty years behind bars, before DNA evidence exonerates them.

What can we change, to cause less crime, and make prisons more effective? Here are a few ideas on the table, none of them my own, but I recommend to both sides of the aisle:

- Increase staffing for all police forces. Ironically, the US has fewer police per person than most of the western world! We need more well-trained, effective police.

- Legalize marijuana nation-wide. There is no use criminalizing something that over 50% of Americans have used, and over 10% have smoked in the past year. Treat it like alcohol and cigarettes, controlled and taxed, but not prohibited.

- Use alternatives to prison for more crimes, where evidence clearly shows better alternatives. These include fines, parole, community service, restricted movements, full house arrest, or other forced changes that fit the crime.

- Eliminate capital punishment, which costs on average $1 million per execution, more than life-in-prison, has no deterrent effect different from life-in-prison, and is proven to have irrevocably punished innocent people.

- Invest the savings from above to social work and crime-prevention programs, and experiments to make prisons more rehabilitating than punitive.

- For all police forces, establish anti-racism rules and training, to reduce the persecution of (in particular) black Americans.

The strongest message I heard from BLM in the summer of 2020 was "defund the police." My first reaction was to scoff, and treat it as hyperbole. I was particularly disgusted by one radical's Instagram post, an ex-friend of a friend: "All cops, yes all, ESPECIALLY the ones related to YOU, are bastards. Fuck the police. Fuck the police forever." I thought I understood the rage, but targeting 100% of the police in the country, and getting rid of all of them, is crazy, right? Common sense says this would mean unbridled robbery, murder, rioting, assaults, rapes, and other crimes.

Then I started reading more considered, fact-based essays about what "defund the police" might mean to more rational people. I think most would agree that we need strong police forces. But some places in the US have poured more and more budget into police departments, while reducing spending on schools, garbage collection, child services, parks, after-school programs, sports, social services, mental health aid, and on and on. There are terrible parts of some towns where police cars roam in great numbers, but there are almost no other government services. We need to revisit the mission and funding and direction we give our police. I believe in a police force that serves and protects, one that almost never kills or hurts anyone, one that fits into a range of public services, including great schools, great health care, clean cities, and help for the needy. Hundreds of years ago, this would be a silly daydream that got you laughed at. Today, this is the normal reality in most rich countries, except the United States. Let's get better.

On September 17, 2022 I was surprised to learn something about American policing. If I had been asked, I would have guessed the US was "over-policed". But no, America spends less on policing than other rich countries: about 0.8% of GDP, compared with 1% in the European Union. Germany has 23% more police officers per person than America; France has 33% more[71]. So while we might need some improvements to training, it's arguable we need increases, not decreases, to our forces.

---

[71] The Economist, Sep 17, 2022

13: GENDER

I didn't want to write this chapter. Do I believe it's a major issue in the US? Absolutely. Laws have been passed and lambasted in the past few years bearing on sex and gender[72]. Court cases and TV shows are dedicated to it. Conservative and liberal extremes are angry with each others' positions on gender issues. My problem is that I haven't got any good answers yet.

Despite being married to a professor of Women's and Gender Studies, I struggle to answer the tough questions being asked about gender today, but perhaps I can make a start to this chapter by at least framing those questions clearly. Maybe I can understand what's making so many people upset about bathrooms and sports competitions, and feel out some directions to eventually reach consensus.

Let's begin with what we might all hope to agree on, some

---

72 "Bathroom Bill" Legislative Tracking, National Conference of State Legislatures

definitions of sex and gender.

Humans are all born with some biological sex. The vast majority of us are either anatomically male, or anatomically female, possessing either balls and a penis, or breasts and a vagina. A small fraction are born with somewhat different anatomies, and these people often face terrible challenges living in societies expecting binary sex.

Gender is a different thing. Gender is the role we play regarding sex... and since sex is such a huge part of being human, gender is usually a huge part of our identity. All human societies have "typical" male and female gender roles very well defined. Boys grow up to be men. They learn to be strong, to provide, to lead. Girls grow up to be women. They learn to be beautiful, to nurture, to submit. Or in some societies, women learn to lead, and men to submit. Societal upbringing determines whether long hair or short hair is masculine or feminine, whether pink or blue is for girls or boys, and which gender should choose the matings.

Ah, the world would be so much simpler if everyone was clearly male or female, both in sex and gender, if every male was attracted only to females, and females only to males, and if all the worlds' societies and all the human beings agreed on the list of gender rules for each sex. But that is not our world, and I said "simpler" not "better". The humanist revolution has given people freedom to be what they choose, and what they feel. Not many Americans feel women should be forced to wear dresses, nor that men should be forced to marry women, although that was practically the case when I was born.

How far should that freedom to do whatever we want be allowed to go? There are areas where the divide in America is deep. Should anyone be allowed to enter any bathroom? Should anyone be allowed to enter any athletic competition? Should we divide bathrooms and sports and anything else by sex or gender or neither? Should children be surgically or chemically altered if they or their parents want to change their sexual organs?

I'd rather not weigh in on the bathroom bills, except

perhaps to wish for a more easygoing future where public washrooms are all unisex for convenience, and for showers or other places where nudity is a norm, private divisions be made so most people are comfortable. Perhaps no rules will work for everyone.

I'll have more to say in future versions of this book, but I think we are years away from reaching consensus on how to organize sports in ways that are fair to all participants. Certainly there should be no discrimination preventing any person from trying out for the top "open" level of any sport, but it's unclear how to regulate other levels. Today in most cases there are divisions of men and women, as well of weight, or skill level, or age. But how to define "women" so that everyone agrees? I don't have an answer, and I'm skeptical of anyone who is certain they do. I'm fond of the proposal to have an "open" category for the top athletes in the world, and a "women's" category for people born biologically female. It's still problematic to many, but it feels to me like a reasonable grouping. It won't make extreme progressives happy.

On sex reassignment surgery, my personal liberal streak advocates for "if you want it, go for it" but I've read enough troubling articles[73] that I favor not allowing it for children. Even for strong cases of gender dysphoria, where children feel they have the wrong bodies for who they are, I think the decision to alter them should wait until they are adults. But that's my personal opinion, and I don't think the evidence is conclusive either way. Which alternative is protecting children from harm? Forcing them to stay with a sex they feel wrong in? Or operating irreversibly in a way they might regret? Either one might be "wrong" for that person in the long run, and it probably depends on the person. Perhaps this is not an area for government to make the decisions, but rather for parents

---

[73] https://en.wikipedia.org/wiki/Sex_reassignment_surgery, and see the April 5, 2023 special issue of The Economist: "The evidence to support medicalized gender transitions in adolescents is worryingly weak"

and children and their doctors together. Until the research is clear, how about we leave it to them?

19: CASH

Money is vital. The US dollar is an essential tool around the world. The US government stands behind the US dollar, and makes sure its value stays strong. Long ago, "cash" was psychologically more real for most people than a number in a bank account. Even longer ago, gold was more real for most people than any other currency. And even longer ago, chickens and cows were more useful as a means of payment than gold. We have come a long way. Cash is a steadily shrinking part of the economy. Just as cows and chickens were not a terrific way to measure value, and gold fell out of use, cash is by now largely useless — except of course for criminals.

I've looked at that last sentence through the prism of my challenge. How might conservative Americans respond? Yes, many criminals rely on cash, but there is also a large population of law-abiding Americans who prefer it, and view cash as a more honest, conservative barter than electronic exchanges. As recently as 2017, the Fed reported cash as the most frequently used payment method in the US, at 30% of transactions. What can I offer those people who still prefer it?

First, I hope they will feel more secure, with banks that the US government stands behind, guaranteeing that their bank balance means they have the money, and nobody can steal it. The "safety" of cash has its limits, as you can lose it, or have it stolen, or most insidious of all, the Fed could potentially allow inflation to destroy its value. Is a bank account better or worse than cash, for these risks? I think the bank account wins on the first two, and gets a draw on the third. It takes time to feel secure though, even if you know rationally that something is safer.

Second, even those who prefer cash may be willing to sacrifice for the good of society. If we can eliminate cash entirely, we can have a huge impact on crime rates, including illegal immigration. There can be no mugging for money, if there is no cash, and every credit card needs a PIN. Some mugger might threaten you to give up your PIN, but even that goes away with better identification systems. Eventually we'll have retinal scans or DNA tests to validate every important transaction.

Cash has another benefit that current alternatives in the US don't offer: the psychological value of carrying a limited amount. I can head to the pub with $50 and my driver's license in my pocket, and feel confident that no matter how stupid I get, I won't spend more than $50. When I go Christmas shopping at the mall, I'm at risk of spending my entire credit limit across multiple credit cards, plus my bank balance ahead of my January mortgage payment, if I don't have the discipline to resist. I'm not speaking hypothetically here; I've been there. There was a time when credit cards were poison for me, and I've sadly seen many other people who suffer from an inability to spend less than their credit limit. If your credit limit is the cash in your wallet, at least you avoid growing debt.

We can build the same psychological tools with electronic money. You can have a digital wallet on your phone, with only $50 available, and go out with that. You can use debit cards instead of credit cards, and limit your debit bank account to a maximum withdrawal per day. Yes, it takes some mental effort and some skill with technology, but I think everybody is capable of what's required. Banks already today impose some such rules. Would it be worth it?

Imagine near elimination of muggings, robberies, illegal drug trade, loan sharks, protection rackets, and black markets. Yes they will find ways to launder electronic money, and continue in some capacity, but they will be far more subject to detection and arrest than cash currently allows them.

The change should not happen overnight. People need time to adapt. Although America is 5-10 years behind other advanced economies in electronic payment, our trend to catch up is well established. One benefit of being behind is that other countries have proven the path, paid the development costs for the new technologies, and shown the cost savings. For example, India established an identification system called the *Aadhaar* ("foundation") over the past couple years, with fingerprints and iris scans, to reduce fraud and get government payments to the right people. Based on the Aadhaar, financial companies in India have developed applications for payments and transfers on mobile phones, which consumers have decided they like better even than credit cards or cash, judging by the trending numbers of transactions for each.

Over the next ten years, it's almost inevitable that cash will decline. Like the shift to sustainable energy, which is now cheaper than coal, it doesn't even require government investment, just that government stay out of the way of progress, although a government-mandated secure personal identification system could help a lot.

Timothy Bult

20: DAYLIGHT SAVING TIME

Eliminate the twice-annual change between daylight savings and standard time; let's end the madness of increased traffic accidents, reduced productivity, extra stress, missed meetings, and sleep disruption, all caused by a change that saved some street light energy in the 19th century[74]. This should be an easy bipartisan win. Seven of ten Americans want to eliminate it (CBS News, November 1, 2019).

A decision remains though: do we keep Standard Time or Daylight Savings Time? I personally don't care, as long as I stop losing an hour of sleep every Spring. The extra hour in Fall just doesn't make up for it.

So what's better, more daylight in the evening (Daylight Savings Time) or the morning (Standard Time)? There is more human activity in the early evening that morning, so the "better" choice for reduced accidents and crime and deaths is Daylight Savings Time. I support that. The only counter argument I've heard is that starting school in the dark is dangerous for kids. That's easily solved. Why should schools start at 8am or even earlier? Kids would be happier and

---

[74] Switching the Clocks Twice a Year Isn't Just Annoying. It's Deadly. NY Times March 8, 2024.

healthier and do better in school if it started later. Why not match school hours closer to office hours, reducing the burden of childcare at the same time?

21: ABORTION

The conflict between "right to life" and "right to choose" divides America like no other issue. I moved this chapter last because it's the hardest to find common ground, even though over 70% of Americans support the position I suggest. I hope that if you've read to this point, we have some mutual understanding and respect, and we can explore this difficult issue with sincerity and an open mind. If you think this issue isn't difficult at all, then I suggest your mind is closed. I sincerely respect those advocates who believe and care deeply that a baby is being killed with every abortion. I also respect those who don't believe a baby is being killed, and want pregnant women to have the choice and medical support to end their pregnancies if they so choose. In most cases, I don't believe this is a conflict between the right to life and the right to choose. Practically every American believes that in general, the right to life trumps the right to choose. I don't get to choose to murder someone who irritates me, even if they invade my space. Their right to life overrides my right to choose. The real question in the abortion debate is about when the right to life should kick in. That said, I'm a man, and it will never happen to me that another human being takes over a part of my body and physically modifies me for nine months, with permanent effects. I understand, when a woman tells me I have no right to tell her what to do about an invasion of her body, especially if she had no say in its conception, or was prevented from using contraception. She might feel as much right to abort the fetus as a man does to shoot a midnight trespasser in his living room, whether the trespasser is an evil invader, or an innocent drunkard stumbling into the wrong house.

Through most of human history, human life was considered to start at birth. In some cultures it started even later, upon naming the child. Modern medicine has made that obsolete. We know that throughout the third trimester, the fetus has a working brain that dreams, a heart that beats, and can even survive without the mother, if someone provides the best medical care available today. The viability of a fetus moves earlier and earlier as medicine advances. It's reasonable to forecast that eventually we will be able to raise a baby entirely outside a mother, from conception onward.

There is a case to be made, to legally define human life, with all its rights and protections under the law, as starting at conception. But is that what all or even most Americans believe? What is the real truth of when life starts? Can we find a shared truth? For a few years, I despaired at finding a proposal that meets my criteria for this book, that both conservatives and liberals can love it, but in 2022, as the Supreme Court threw the decision back to the states, I read what the majority of Americans want, left and right: legal abortion in the first trimester, and restrictions on abortion thereafter[75].

The US Supreme Court has not weighed in on when life begins, directly, although they have indeed ruled on when life ends, applying the Harvard Medical School's definition of

---

[75] https://www.vox.com/policy-and-politics/23167397/abortion-public-opinion-polls-americans -- "85 percent of American voters think abortion should be legal in some or all circumstances"

"brain death". Essentially, humans are still alive if their brain is working, and dead if it's not. The Roe vs. Wade precedent was set with lots of reference to fetal viability, as if that was a useful definition of life. I don't think it is.

As the best definition, one I think the majority of Americans believe in, I recommend we pass laws, or that the Supreme Court decide, applying the same standard for human life at the beginning as we already use consistently at its end: brain activity. There is no functioning brain in a fetus before approximately 13 weeks, and hence no human life, in the sense of a legal person with human rights. If you have no brain, you have no soul. The sacred right to life starts when you have a soul – when you have a brain that can support it. By this understanding, first-trimester abortion doesn't kill a human being any more than a couple's decision to not have sex kills their potential child. I would support laws defining human life to start when brain activity begins, with concomitant full support to provide all women with access to abortion until that time.

An extremist "right to life" minority in America tends to believe life starts at conception. Some of them view the morning-after pill as murder. They see the value of a fertilized egg as more important than the quality of life, privacy, health, or happiness of the mother. From laws they have passed, they would rather a teen mother raped by her father have a life of misery and poverty, including a miserable life for the child, than allow doctors to abort the fertilized egg. On the other hand, the "right to choose" group tends to ignore the question of human life's beginnings. Based on some extreme positions allowing abortion even when the fetus is viable, they use an ancient, obsolete view of human life starting at birth, or they put the woman's right to rid her body of an invader ahead of the invader's right to life. In a modern society that values human life, and abhors infanticide, this to me is equally wrong as those who fight the morning-after pill. Can we not strive to agree on a rational definition of the beginning of life?

America as a society needs to reach consensus on that

beginning, when the right to life of a new human being comes into force, overriding the mother's right to do what she likes with her own body.

I think we can all agree that fewer abortions would be a good thing, as would unwanted pregnancies in general. Let's visit policies toward those ends.

From The Economist on January 4, 2020: "Texas is a poster-child for abstinence education." Texas law requires teaching to emphasize abstinence 'as the preferred choice of behavior in relationship to all sexual activity for unmarried persons of school age.' But over 60% of Texan high-school seniors say they have had sex. According to the Centers for Disease Control and Prevention, Texan teens are the least likely in America to have used contraception the last time they did. In other words, propaganda to prevent sex leads to more abortions. If you really want to stop abortions, improving sex education is a great start.

For an opposite experience, look at Delaware. I pull from the same March 5, 2020 issue of The Economist for the following facts. From 2014 to 2019 Delaware trained primary health-care workers regularly to ask each woman of childbearing age about birth control, and get them contraception if they wanted it. Births following unintended pregnancies fell by 25% in the first three years. The abortion rate dropped more sharply than in any other state in America.

With an American consensus definition of the beginning of life, and policies to educate our youth, we can reduce abortions in America to a tiny number, and early enough that none will be murder.

22: SUMMARY

I started writing this book before Covid-19 struck. During my months of writing and rewriting, sharing drafts with conservative and liberal friends, refining the ideas, the world transformed, and then transformed again.

Before World War Two, the US government's total spending was about 5% of GDP[76]. The war saw it soar to 25%. Then an interesting thing happened. It never went down. Today US government spending remains about 25% of GDP, until 2020 and 2021 saw it soar with stimulus packages.

Will the same thing happen after the war on Covid-19?

Whether government spending in this country or others jumps permanently or not, there is a refreshed need for innovative political action and good decisions. Good ideas, for increased or decreased spending, increased or decreased taxation, are more vital than ever, to rebuild in the wake of this disaster, to act out of love. Why do I say love? I mean this in the Christian sense of love for all fellow humans. The governments we create are one of the most important ways we express our core values, what we decide to collectively protect, where and how we spend our money, what we love and will sacrifice to support.

---

[76] The Economist, "Building up the pillars of state", March 28, 2020.

Writing this book has made me think about what it means to be conservative or liberal, particularly in the US. It's fascinating how the definitions have changed over the centuries, as well as the allegiance of parties. Liberal used to mean freedom from government interference, and is indeed used as a label for right wing parties in many other countries. The Democrats used to be the conservative party in the US, while the Republican Party, founded in Yankee north Wisconsin, started specifically to oppose the oppression of blacks by slavery. But that's just historical curiosity. What matters more is how you will vote in the next election, what drives someone to choose Democrat or Republican, or to abstain, or vote in protest for a no-hope candidate.

One thing that gives me hope is the large majorities of Americans that actually agree on the biggest issues in this country, even if Congress ignores those majority opinions. This book tries to appeal to those strong majority positions. I'm trying to find solutions that don't get labeled liberal or conservative, and can stand simply as American. I'm not naively saying there are no serious differences in American opinion, but I am saying there is room for common ground.

Let's remember these political labels are simplifications, and Americans really should not be lumped together into two or three political categories. Sure, most conservatives will say God's will should apply in all things, and most liberals will say every person in the US should get to vote as easily as going to the store, but I doubt you can find two Americans that agree down to every detailed policy position on every issue. There are not two camps in US politics; there are 300 million camps, more or less close to each other. And on most of the big issues, a big majority of Americans are in favor of certain policies. Let's try to get past the labels, and implement more of those majority solutions.

Here is a table of the key suggestions I make in this book, along with at least one reason for conservatives and liberals to love each one.

Issue	Suggestion	For conservatives to love	For liberals to love
Military Spending	Maintain at current share of GDP.	Maintain overwhelming superiority over potential enemies.	Maintain power to support our values worldwide.
Oil and Coal	No more subsidies, spend the savings on tax cuts and research.	Reduced government interference, let the free market decide energy.	Save the planet by delaying global warming enough for cheaper renewable energy to take over.
Health Care	Just like car insurance.	Free market, no government health care.	Health care for all.
Right to bear arms	Make guns like cars, where Americans can buy as many as they like, with appropriate training and license.	Affirm the Second Amendment.	Licensing and safety requirements that reduce gun deaths to the levels of Canada or Europe.
Taxes	1.9% federal sales tax.	Balanced budget without cutting the military or social security.	Balanced budget.
Regulation Overload	Strengthen the "1 rule in, 2 rules out" idea and assess	Steadily decrease the overall amount of federal regulation.	Prioritize regulation to improve Americans'

	financial impact long term.		standard of living and environmental quality.
Fake News	Require all media to apply the Wikipedia model.	All lies get exposed.	All lies get exposed.
Education	Federal subsidy to raise all schools' funding to a minimum standard.	Better educated workforce, a key demand of businesses for future prosperity.	Better education for currently disadvantaged children.
Student Loans and Tuition	Tuition and loan payments as % of income.	No free ride.	Equal access to all.
Immigration	Tougher ID and family immigration rules, higher quotas for work-based immigrants.	Tougher on illegal entry, while increasing immigration that directly benefits the economy.	Clear path for fair treatment of all claimants, from refugees to illegal residents.
Voting Rights	Universal ID system guaranteeing one vote for each person, and independent agency for electoral boundaries.	Regain America's moral leadership of the world's democracies.	A fair voice for every citizen.
Allies and Enemies	Friendship extended on	Tougher treatment of those	Support for human rights

	basis of US values.	who oppose US values.	and other US values.
Foreign Aid	Strengthen military and economic alliance with all democratic countries.	US leadership for fundamental rights: free markets, personal freedoms, free press, independent judiciary.	Uphold democratic values worldwide.
Social Security	Replace by UBI.	Less bureaucracy for the same benefits.	Secure benefits for all Americans.
Racism and CRT	Priority on equality of education.	Equality of opportunity for all Americans.	Equality of opportunity for all Americans.
Crime	Less prison, more rehab, more police, more training.	Reduced crime	More humane treatment
Gender	Sex reassignment for adults only	No radical legislation	Freedom to do as you please, when adult
Cash	Eliminate.	Reduced crime. Lower costs for American business.	Reduced crime.
Daylight Savings Time	Stop changing twice a year.	Lower cost for American business.	Less suffering for American people.
Abortion	Life starts as it ends, with brain activity.	Sanctity of life applied to abortion law.	Guaranteed access all of first trimester.

I hope the ideas I put forward in this little book are of some use in making America's future even greater. If you think so, please consider some of the following actions:

1. Vote. If you are American, and if you like the ideas in this book, vote for the candidates most likely to implement them.

2. Rate this book on Goodreads or Amazon http://www.amazon.com/review/create-review?&asin=B08KKZ4GG5. Please write a review; it can be just a few words of what you liked or disliked. The more and higher ratings this book gets, the more people will read it.

3. If you really love the ideas, make them your own, and promote them yourself. Send a copy of this book to your favorite politician, or write your own.

4. Send me feedback to improve a later edition, or to inspire another book.

5. Connect with me on www.TimothyBult.com or social media. Request being put on my newsletter, to hear about other books I'm publishing.

23: READING LIST

I've tried to provide convincing and interesting references for every possibly contentious factual claim in this book. This led me to read a lot of books and a lot of articles from a lot of media, and indeed to modify some of my earlier opinions.

I recommend the following in particular, not always that I agree with all their ideas, but because they provide fascinating real data and perspectives. For the issues covered in this book, I consider these essential reading:

1. The Economist. There are many high-quality newspapers and magazines constantly analyzing the state of the world. The Economist is my favorite. If they have a bias, it is for scientific facts and old fashioned liberal values.

2. Enlightenment Now, by Steven Pinker. This is the best antidote for pessimism about the world. Pinker proves with masses of compelling data how enlightenment values, that is the liberal values underpinning America,

have dramatically improved the world and continue to do so.

3. Losing Control: How a left-right coalition blocked immigration reform and provoked the backlash that elected Trump, by Jerry Kammer.

4. Principles for Dealing with the Changing World Order: Why Nations Succeed and Fail, by Ray Dalio. Most investors are happy to analyze data and trends of the past few decades. Ray Dalio surveys the last 2000 years, looking at how the world's most powerful nations over that time (China, Spain, the Netherlands, Britain, and America, in that order) have risen and fallen. He's built a fascinating model for what causes the rises and falls. While I disagree with his conclusion that an ascendant China is about to supplant a declining US, his research and reasoning are fascinating.

5. Economic Facts and Fallacies, Thomas Sowell. Again a book I disagree with vehemently on many points, but really made me think. Sowell's a famous conservative who effectively criticizes "woke" theories, with extensive fact-checking. I think he's wrong on feminism and academia and some other topics, but he has much useful to say about poverty, foreign aid, and the improvement of black people's lot in the US.

6. Cynical Theories: How Activist Scholarship Made Everything about Race, Gender, and Identity — and Why This Harms Everybody. By Helen Pluckrose and James Lindsay. I was interested to learn why Critical Race Theory has so incensed American conservatives. Those I read or listened to were mostly lying or utterly mistaken about what CRT means and does. This book provides facts and cogent explanations of where CRT and related "wokism" have gone too far.

7. The Political Centrist, John Lawrence Hill. This political scientist sketches the history of Liberalism and Conservatism, and makes a valiant effort to define the essence of each, as well as a "Centrist" position in the

US. It helped me understand US liberals and conservatives better than I did, along with the crazy zigzag history of the two terms. I recommend it especially for its later chapters on the issues, such as abortion, where it provides an insightful history.

8. Unsettled: What Climate Science Tells Us, What It Doesn't, and Why It Matters, by Steven E Koonin. This former Chief Scientist of BP Oil claims not to be a climate change denier, but sets out to deny the main points of climate change science. He accuses the media of cherry-picking facts to dramatize global warming, while he stands accused of cherry-picking facts to deny its importance. Just as I advocate reading Fox News as well as CNN, to avoid having blinkers, I suggest reading Koonin as well as the reviews that point out his errors. One of many interesting finds on careful read of Unsettled is that even he acknowledges global warming caused by CO_2 is real, that (for example) global summer snow cover is shrinking as a result, and that ocean temperatures are rising dangerously.

ACKNOWLEDGMENTS

Many thanks to my early readers, several of whom sent me a wealth of information and critiques and questions, which have led me to increase the references, accuracy, and balance. A special thanks to Ron, whose questions and criticism and demand for "the facts" have greatly improved this book.

I hope my readers will further fact-check me and help me correct any errors.

ABOUT THE AUTHOR

Timothy Bult was born in the mountains of British Columbia, Canada, to Dutch immigrants Roelof & Ineke. He grew up skiing, camping, reading novels, in love with all the humanities and most of the sciences. After high school he moved to Vancouver for college. He spent a year in France to obtain a Master's in Computer Science, then returned for a Master's in Artificial Intelligence research at the University of British Columbia. He did industrial AI work at Bell-Northern Research in Ottawa for three years before returning to BC yet again to work at MacDonald Dettwiler Associates (MDA), in systems engineering around the world. After 27 years in Vancouver, visiting China, Israel, most of the United States, and pockets of the Middle East & Europe, he moved to Milwaukee.

Timothy works at large companies managing global business transformations. While much of his writing is either classified or proprietary, he has published articles and books in various genres: science fiction, politics, AI, leadership, and romance.

Thank you so much for reading this book. Please leave a review wherever you obtained it, or on www.TimothyBult.com – and get a free e-poster copy of The Keys To Happiness: